RESILIENT

The Power to Get Back Up!

Presented by

Dr. Cheryl Wood

and Resilient Women Around the World

RESILIENT: THE POWER TO GET BACK UP
Copyright © 2023 Presented by Dr. Cheryl Wood

Published by MYJOY Publishing House

ISBN: 979-8-3507-2044-0
Kindle ISBN: 979-8-3507-2045-7

Table of Contents

Table of Contents

Table of Contents

Table of Contents

Foreword

By Dr. Chere M. Goode

Life's journey can be a rollercoaster. Sometimes it can be full of joy and happiness, but other times, it can be full of great sadness, depression, confusion, anxiety, hopelessness, hurt, and anger. It is normal to experience one or all of those emotions in life. Don't beat yourself up. Embrace those feelings and give yourself permission to feel whatever you feel during your journey. Take as long as you need to regroup. However, the worst thing you can do is stay stuck in negative feelings for too long. You may ask, why? Well, those feelings can fester and become your new norm, which would harm your mental and physical well-being. You can be resilient and shift those feelings into something positive. Turn your pain and disappointments into purpose and find the strength to rise up in the midst of life's ups and downs.

This book will aid you in getting back up and being resilient. The authors in this book have shared their real-life examples of finding inner strength and not allowing what has altered their life plan to hold them back even while some were at the lowest points in their lives.

When I lost my 20-year-old son, Jordan Alexander Cofield, in a tragic motorcycle accident on August 22, 2020, followed by his father's death just 6 months later, my life drastically changed forever. The hardest thing after my losses was to get up and continue with my life. I did not want to go on. I felt all the emotions mentioned above at some point or another. Some days, I felt all those emotions in one day. The flooding of emotions had me questioning my sanity. It was like being on a rollercoaster ride for many days with the ups and downs of my emotions. I had to choose either getting swallowed up by my grief and pain or affecting the world by being resilient and getting back up.

I started creating positive initiatives and purpose out of my painful tragedies. I went into immediate action to keep my son's memory alive. I built up a determination to never allow all the positive things my Jordan had done in his short time on this earth to go to waste. I went into action amid my grief and healing. My mission was to ensure my son's name, legacy, and memory were never forgotten. I turned my sadness and grief into resilience, strength, and positivity by adopting a roadway in my son's honor, starting a scholarship fund in his honor, and starting a 501c3 no-profit organization. Those initiatives in my late son's honor kept me busy and fueled me to keep living a life of purpose. It feels good to know Jordan will never be forgotten, and his legacy will now enrich the lives of others.

I encourage every reader of this book to dig deep within and find those things that bring you strength, happiness, joy, and purpose, then nurture those things as you heal from whatever or whoever tried to keep you down. The main thing is to keep getting up! Getting back up is a choice. If it were easy to get back up, everyone would do it. The road to resilience will not be easy, but it is necessary. Someone is always watching your journey and drawing the strength to get back up because they saw you get up. Your resilience gives hope and proof that life continues after unexpected occurrences happen.

Dr. Chere M. Goode

Dr. Chere M. Goode is the Founder/CEO of Total Harmony Enterprises, Make Me Over Wellness, and the Jordan Alexander Cofield Foundation (a 501c3 nonprofit organization dedicated to her late son). Goode has been a Licensed Practical Nurse for over 30 years and is Nationally Certified in Hospice and Palliative Care. She is a 10x #1 Amazon International Best- Selling Author, Speaker, Coach, Founder of the annual RECHARGE Health, Wellness and Fitness Expo, and an Ambassador/Spokesperson for the American Heart & Stroke Association.

Best known as the RECHARGE Strategist, Goode teaches professional women strategies for self-care to recharge their mental, physical, and emotional batteries for success in life and business. Goode has been featured on ABC, Dr. Oz, Wendy Williams, Baltimore's TV 25, Society Moms TV, Radio One, WOLB Radio, The Baltimore Times and SpeakerCon, to name a few. She has received numerous awards and Government citations for tenacity in business. Goode's expertise in the areas of RECHARGE strategies, stress management, self-care, wellness, and heart disease prevention has impacted the lives of men and women globally.

Introduction

By Dr. Cheryl Wood

Visionary of RESILIENT! The Power to Get Back Up
International Empowerment Speaker | TEDx Speaker |
Best-Selling Author | Executive Speaker Coach | Leadership
Expert

No matter where you go in the world, you will find resilient women who have defied the odds and made a choice to get back up from some of life's most gut-wrenching and unexpected challenges. Every woman you meet has untold stories of trauma, trials, obstacles and setbacks she has faced in her life. Although women get knocked down, we refuse to stay down. There are bold, courageous, resilient women worldwide who are fighters, warriors and conquerors. There are women who commit to doing whatever it takes to emerge as a victor over everything that tries to break her. This book will give you a glimpse into the lives and stories of some of the most resilient women in the world.

RESILIENT! The Power to Get Back Up is a powerful compilation of raw, authentic stories of women who chose to get back up. In this book, you will get an exclusive, up-close-and-personal seat to hear the personal testimonies that have emerged from the tests they've endured. Their stories of bouncing back when life had counted them out will pull at your heartstrings and inspire you to claim power over every challenge you face. This powerful collection of stories shows the bold, tenacious, and resilient spirit of women who refuse to throw in the towel even when the going gets tough. They show the truth in the adage, "What doesn't kill you makes you stronger."

I celebrate each of the co-authors of this project for boldly sharing their truth – the good, the bad, the messy, the uncertain, the breakdowns, and the breakthroughs. Each story unveils the co-author's unique struggles and how she shifted her mindset, attitude, and actions to press through to victory.

As you immerse yourself in the stories of RESILIENT! The Power to Get Back Up, you will be reminded that no tribulation can hold you back from fulfilling your destiny unless you give it permission to. The stories will reignite a fire inside of you to persevere through anything meant to break you because there's always something greater on the other side of the temporary pain you will experience amid challenges. The co-authors show you firsthand how to become a beautiful diamond under extreme pressure.

On my journey, I had to discover that I could be a victor over anything life threw my way. As a young girl raised in poverty in Lafayette housing project in Baltimore, Maryland, I had to work to change my toxic thinking about obstacles and setbacks. I decided that I would not be a victim of my environment or any negative circumstances I faced. Instead, I chose a course of resilience over anything that tried to impede my progress and advancement toward success. Whether it was the season of my life when I went through the humiliation of bankruptcy, the trauma of divorce, or the grief of losing my father, I refused to stay down. And every time I decided to be resilient instead of throwing in the towel, afterward, I was so grateful for the experiences because they made me more aware of who I was and whose I was. Every challenge I endured helped me to build character, develop increased confidence, become more tenacious, and learn who my true support system was. I thank God for giving me the strength to bounce back from every challenge that knocked me down. He brought me through my most difficult life challenges. And every co-author in this book has shown the same resilient spirit, which is why they are courageously and vulnerably sharing their stories and their truth to inspire you.

After reading the stories in this book, you will feel more inspired, empowered, determined, and committed than ever before to keep pressing through your journey even in the face of every challenge, obstacle, setback, trial or tribulation. And, most importantly, to be reminded that as each of the co-authors has chosen a path of resilience, you can too. You are strong, powerful, tenacious, and resilient!

Dr. Cheryl Wood
Visionary of RESILIENT! The Power to Get Back Up
WEBSITE: www.cherylempowers.com
EMAIL: info@cherylwoodempowers.com
SOCIAL MEDIA: @CherylEmpowers

Dr.Cheryl Wood

Dr. Cheryl Wood is an International Keynote Speaker, 2x TEDx Presenter, Best Selling Author, Public Speaking Coach, and CEO of Global Speakers University, a training and development company that equips entrepreneurs, executives, and leaders with the tools to maximize their impact through the art of effective communication and public speaking. Wood has delivered riveting keynotes for NASA, Verizon, Prudential, Capital One, U.S. Department of Defense, U.S. Department of Agriculture, the FBI, The United Nations, Federally Employed Women, Blacks In Government, and a host of prestigious law firms, corporations, and international conferences.

Wood has coached entrepreneurs and leaders around the world to exponentially increase their impact and influence by helping them to polish their stage presence, increase their platform confidence, and develop transformational messages that move audiences into decisive action to produce desired results. Wood has been featured in Forbes Magazine, Huffington Post, Rolling Out, Sheen, Essence, Black Enterprise, ABC News, Fox 5 News, Fox 45 News, Good Morning Washington, and The Washington Informer. She is the recipient of the 2024 ICON of Excellence Award, the 2021 President's Lifetime Achievement Award, and the 2019 GODSU Honorary Doctorate of Humane Letters for over a decade of helping leaders globally to unleash and amplify the power of their voices.

Quitting Isn't an Option

By Debra Bell-Campbell

"Courage doesn't always roar. Sometimes courage is the quiet voice at the end of the day saying, 'I will try again tomorrow.'"
Mary Anne Radmacher

I navigate uncharted waters in a world that often celebrates extroversion and quick decision-making. Characterized by introspection and a preference for solitude, I am misunderstood and undervalued, leading some to question my ability to succeed in high-pressure roles. Over the years, I have learned to lean into my hidden strength – the power of resilience.

Resilience grew out of the need to survive. I grew up in the traditional home where my mom stayed at home, and my daddy got the opportunity to work full-time to support team Bell. Our house was noisy, and the only way you got noticed was if you were the oldest, the youngest, the naughtiest, the nicest, or the smartest. You guessed it; I wasn't any of those. It was difficult for me to establish my identity. I often had feelings of not being good enough and doubting my abilities. However, these feelings grew with me and forced me to ask where I fit because giving up was not an option. Fitting in and finding my voice would merely be a matter of timing.

The timing was thrust upon me without warning. Eight months after my mother's ascension, my dad was gone just like that. It was Friday, August 7, 2015. I arrived at my childhood home the night before and could not wait to see my daddy, son, and everyone else. I rushed into the house and went straight to my daddy's bedroom, where he was lying on the bed facing the wall. At first, I thought he was asleep, so I ran to greet him. Although he was not sleeping, he did not turn to face me while we talked.

The next day, I sprang to my feet as I heard my sister Carol's chilling scream. I ran into the living room, where I saw my dad slumped in his favorite rocking chair. The house was noisy, and I could not hear myself think, yet my training kicked in. I immediately told Carol to call 911, yelled to another sister to take all the kids across the street, then instructed my nephews to get my dad out of the chair and onto the floor. There, I performed CPR on my dad until emergency services arrived. I knew he was gone way before the paramedics arrived, and I kept doing cycles of 30 compressions and two breaths. As I continued to breathe life into him, I had flashes of all the times we laughed together, and most of who I am is him. I felt the urgency to resuscitate my own life. At that moment, I realized that I couldn't hide anymore. This was the first time in my life I felt like I showed up when it mattered the most. I was visible!

This untimely event gut-punched me. It hit me like a ton of bricks. I felt like time was running out, and I had not become the woman I was raised to be. What was keeping me from "becoming"? My inability to embrace my hidden strengths was holding me back.

Being an introverted woman in leadership can be challenging. However, your unique strengths can help you thrive because quitting is not an option. Here are strategies I have used to be resilient:

1. Embrace and Leverage My Introverted Strengths
   Introverts often excel in deep thinking, empathy, active listening, and strategic planning. It's essential to embrace these traits and recognize them as valuable assets.

2. Set Boundaries and Prioritize Self-Care:
   Resilience is built on a foundation of emotional and physical well-being, so ensuring they have the space to recharge will enable them to stay focused and effective in their roles.

3. Build a Supportive Network:
   Seek professional organizations or communities that cater to introverted leaders, where they can exchange experiences and strategies for success and eliminate feelings of isolation.

Resilience is not just about weathering challenges; it's also about learning and growing from them. By embracing your introverted nature, setting boundaries, and building a support network, introverted career women can develop a strong foundation for resilience and succeed in their professional and personal endeavors. Faced with adversity and societal expectations, quitting is not an option for introverted leaders. The journey may be challenging, but we defy stereotypes and carve our path to success through our resilience and determination.

Connect with me on social media @dbellcampbell.

Debra Bell-Campbell

Debra Bell-Campbell has been the Owner of Inspired Visions Consulting Group, LLC since 2013 and the co-owner of 2Paths1Leader, LLC since 2022. She has provided essential strategies to help introverted career women learn to leverage their introversion and promote from frontline leadership into mid-level leadership positions.

Debra has authored and published six best-selling books. She co-authored three of the six books with Dr. Les Brown and Dr. Cheryl Wood. In 2022, she was recognized as one of the top ten authors in 2022. Finally, as an international speaker, she received the first annual EPSY awarded by the National Academy of Professional Speakers, Authors, and Coaches (NAPSAC). She has been featured in many conferences, magazines, podcasts, and mainstream news outlets, such as ABC, NBC, and CBS, providing empowerment tips, techniques, and tools for introverted career women in leadership.

Overcome Trauma by Valuing Yourself

By JJ Conway

"Life begins at the end of your comfort zone."
John Maxwell

It's hard to describe my upbringing in a balanced way. Although I know there were some good times (Mom has pictures to prove it), abuse is woven through my memories until my mom left my dad when I was thirteen. Though Mom reared us to be independent, my psyche was already programmed to accept emotional and physical abuse as normal. Besides, a girl usually wants to please her daddy, and my father was as old-world islander as my mom was independent feminist.

I had two boyfriends in college: the first went to jail for assault and the other I dated for three years. I ended the relationship when he became too controlling, but I yielded to family pressure to marry him anyway. "After all," one of my close female family members said, "no one else is barking up your tree, and you don't want to end up old and alone."

Our marriage quickly deteriorated into controlling and abusive behavior. After four years, I tried to leave, but abusing a wife was legal in our state. And back then, a "divorce without cause" would cause them to remove my top-secret security clearance and be grounds for losing my job.

And he knew it.

I foolishly thought I could "love" him back to his old self. I knew my best friend was there somewhere: he volunteered at church, was friendly with the neighbors, and sweet-talked the ladies at the grocery store. If I would "just" stop being so selfish and needy and be a good enough wife,

19

I thought he'd return to being my best friend (not this monster in front of me). These faulty beliefs kept me trapped.

The one bright light from that relationship is my first son. It took eight years and several losses to finally hold this miracle baby in my arms. I looked into his eyes and knew I had to leave so he wouldn't grow up to treat women like his father did.

I volunteered for a six-month military trip to get space and create a plan. I hoped my absence would shake some sense into him. Instead, I came home from that trip to find my house sold and most of my belongings thrown out. We signed divorce papers five days later, and I was now a single military mom with over $845,000 of divorce debt.

On the one hand, life was tough, and I used a lot of cardboard boxes for furniture. But on the other hand, I was free from fifteen years of abuse I had tried to hide from the rest of the world.

When I finally started dating again, I seemed to only attract predators! I still felt unworthy of nice things, nice people, and nice experiences, but it was a huge step forward that I could at least recognize these men would tear down all I had built up financially and professionally. This was another step forward: valuing myself enough to protect myself.

The more I valued myself, the more I attracted abundance into my life: abundant finances, friendships, and abundant fruit in community work and a ministry I started.

They say, "The sexiest thing a woman can put on is confidence," and I started attracting higher-caliber men. Unfortunately, I couldn't get past my past. When a man's mannerisms (in any way) were reminiscent of my dad or ex-husband, I dropped him! I was never going to NEED a man again.

Want? Sure.

Need? Never!

One man broke through my defenses and built a friendship—a partnership—with me. We called or skyped each other every night for almost three years until we married.

Mr. Man (I affectionally call him) carried me through deployments in the Middle East, debilitating car accidents, and the roller coaster of starting my own business. His strengths make up for my many weaknesses, and he meets most of my emotional needs just by being himself.

When I look at the pain and sorrow of the first part of my life, I realize that the last amazing 12 years have been worth every tear I've shed. It's never too late to start over. It's never too late to love yourself. It's never too late to have the experiences you dream of. It's never too late if you're willing to take the first step. And that first step is making the decision today to take ownership of your own life.

JJ Conway

Lieutenant Colonel (retired) JJ Conway was the first Black to serve as a physicist in the Air Force, despite being told by the Air Force, "Blacks can't do physics." After returning from a 6-month military trip, JJ became a financial planner to discover her house sold, divorce papers, and over $845,000 debt to her name. Adapting to life as a military single mom, JJ learned how money worked and how to make it work for her quickly yet ethically.

She now teaches others the same personal growth and financial management skills that let her dump that debt and begin building wealth. She also mirrors these principles when working with technical leaders to improve processes, people, and profit.

LinkTree: https://linktr.ee/jjconway
Instagram: http://instagram.com/JJKnowsTheWay
Facebook: https://www.facebook.com/groups/BuildWealthWithJJ
Linked in: https://linkedin.com/in/JJKnowsTheWay
YouTube: http://www.youtube.com/c/JJKnowsTheWay

It's Time To Delete It, Lovebug

By Teri Donelson

"Strength does not come from winning. Your struggles develop your strengths. When you go through hardships and decide not to surrender, that is strength."
Arnold Schwarzenegger

Here I am waking up 6 AM, still dark outside, grabbing the biggest pots and running across the street to Ms. Pearl's house. She sends me and my two older siblings out back so we can fill our containers with water. Then we slowly take the water filled buckets back across the street, dodging the traffic, at 7, 12 and 13 years old!

This lasted months because my mama, raising eight children alone, couldn't afford to pay the water bill, so we had to do what we had to do. This was my life, so I promised myself I would NOT be poor when I grew up. I did everything "right," graduated high school, went to college, secured a good job, got married, had a baby, but yet life began to life, and it all went to hell real fast.

Depression is a sneaky beast. It comes in different forms, and I didn't realize I was depressed. I lost my Mama, house, job, husband, and nearly my mind. After I had my second child, I gained so much weight I was nearly 300 pounds. I realized how unhappy and unfulfilled I was after looking back over that period. I was living a life based on my mama's expectations of me and not living in my true purpose. Living in an assignment that didn't belong to me, I realized I didn't know what I wanted to do. I lived my life becoming good at stuff, on autopilot, making sure I would never be broke, chasing the paper so far away from what made me happy.

Many people ask me, "How did you get from Chief Operating Officer (COO) of a non-profit organization to one of the founders and COO of one of the largest privately owned fitness companies?" Simply put, I started with my mindset. Many of you reading this may think I NEED to know how to pivot. Let's explore the steps I took to come out of my depressive state and move toward living in my purpose. It wasn't easy, it was a chaLLEnge, but I had to rid myself of the LLE to pivot. Here are my Tee Tips.

L-LIES

Everything on earth has a purpose, and we were born with an assignment for our life. Somewhere along the way, something happened, events occurred that caused a pivot from our purpose. So we tell ourselves lies, things we have heard others say: how can you run a business when you don't have a business degree, how are you going to start a fitness brand and you don't fit the beauty standard? Your first step is to let go of those limited beliefs, that tells you why you can't, and begin to visualize how you WILL. Speak positivity to yourself every day to drown out those lies.

L-LAZINESS

I know you think you want to rest, but sometimes we need to move. Procrastination can be a sign that you just don't know where to start or are feeling overwhelmed, so you just stop moving and sit. I was there, even when I couldn't see the end of the road, I saw a path, so I just continued to move. I didn't know exactly where to turn, but I continued to move. I ran into some bumps, but I continued to move. Moving causes momentum, and each step gets you closer and closer to your destination…. to living in your purpose. My tip for beating laziness is to create your goals and add deadlines. Why do we add deadlines? Because it holds us accountable. Write it down and make those goals measurable and make them realistic.

E-EGO

You must be open to accepting guidance from others. When I pivoted, I didn't know what I was doing. I was driving down a dark path with no roadmap. That's when I found a coach that provided guidance. The road was still mine to travel, but I was given a roadmap that made the process manageable and realistic. That's what a coach/mentor does for you: someone to talk to when those lies foster old habits, holding me accountable when I get lazy. I wasn't alone anymore on this journey. Now, it doesn't STOP the twists and turns of the journey, but I have someone who understands.

By deleting the LLE, that challenge becomes the change you need to pivot, walk and thrive in your purpose.

Teri Donelson

Teri Donelson, affectionately known as "Your Purpose Pusher,' trains aspiring entrepreneurs worldwide to overcome obstacles, pursue passions, and live a life of purpose. She is CEO and Founder of Purpose Chasing Academy, a global company that empowers women to create the best version of themselves and become purposeful in developing a vision and achieving goals. Teri also serves as the COO and a founder of Xtreme Hip Hop, a global fitness company that inspires people to have fun while becoming healthy.

Teri is a visionary recognized for her leadership, commitment, and contributions to her community and the next generation. Her work has been featured on prominent media platforms such as ABC, NBC, FOX, and CBS and in podcasts and magazines. Teri is a mother of two beautiful children, a graduate of the University of Texas and John Carroll University and a member of Delta Sigma Theta Sorority Inc.

Bound by Fear, Free by Faith

By Mona Gray, CPLC, MBA

"If the Son therefore shall make you free, ye shall be free indeed."
John 8:36

How does someone grow up with many talents but remain so afraid to apply them to their life? As an adult, I asked myself this question to take the steps to combat the fear I was living with, so I could become who I would be and finally live out my dreams.

Growing up, I daydreamed daily about what I would be as an adult. I knew I would make the best news anchor there was, and no one could tell me anything different. I practiced how to articulate my words, look professional on camera, achieve stellar writing techniques, and master my people skills. Owning these skills would let me become so successful as a news anchor that my family would be proud, and I would break the negative thoughts that crept into my mind when I was alone. And being an only child meant I was alone – a lot.

Raised by an alcoholic grandmother, I was abused daily as a child. In the morning, I would leave for school, and everything would feel normal – however, by the time I got home in the afternoon, the abuse began. In her eyes, I could do nothing right. If I spoke too loudly, a glass would fly at my head. If I ate too quickly, I was locked in the dark basement. I had to sit and study for hours while my cousins played outside. If I didn't get an A on all my tests, there was a belt, switch, or extension cord with my name on it. And along with the physical abuse, there was mental abuse. I had daily thoughts I wasn't good enough and would never succeed at anything. The verbal and mental abuse affected me so deeply that believing in myself was nonexistent. I became insecure and timid.

By the time my grandmother died, I had given up on dreaming. I was too afraid to dream. I had no one to encourage me to keep pushing and say, "It's never too late" or "Don't give up." So, I went on with my life, acquiring the skills I needed to get by because I wanted to have a decent life for my three children. But I wasn't happy. I let the fear of never being good enough take residence in my heart and my mind. I sabotaged every opportunity I was given and expected the minimum in life. Until one day, I heard a still, small voice whisper, "I did not give you the spirit of fear." I knew that voice in my heart, even though I was never taken to church or read the Bible. I knew someone kept a fire lit in me even when I blew it out.

Although my childhood dream has changed, I know my purpose. I empower others to identify limiting beliefs, examine those beliefs and eliminate negativity while encouraging them to achieve the goals they put on hold out of fear. My faith in God has led me to combat fear and become a successful life coach, transformational speaker, and podcast host.

Do you find it difficult to live your dreams or reach your goals because you live in fear? Here are a few steps to help you overcome this:

1. Be honest about what it is you fear. If you are dishonest with yourself, it will be difficult to face this fear and let it go.

2. Write down and meditate on every scripture about fear. In the Bible, many people lived in fear, but God heard their prayers and delivered them.

3. PRAY. Prayer is the communication tool that lets us speak directly to our Father. Use it to discuss what you fear and let Him comfort you.

4. Live by Faith and let fear GO! Hebrews 11:6 says, "and without faith it is impossible to please God," while 2 Timothy 1:7 says, "For God did not give us the spirit of fear, but of power, and of love, and of a sound mind."

Living in fear robs you of your dreams. Don't let fear be the reason you don't shine and reach your future goals. Let go of the fear that others have placed over your life and live a fruitful, fearless life on purpose!

Mona Gray

Mona Gray is a certified life coach and transformational speaker with a passion for empowering others. As the owner of Clear The Gray Coaching, Mona creates a safe and nurturing environment for clients to identify and eliminate limiting beliefs while guiding them toward their goals. Additionally, Mona serves as a community liaison in the mental health and substance abuse field, showing her dedication to making a difference. With her love for helping people discover their true potential, Mona's passion shines through in her work.

She inspires transformative change, using her warm and compassionate approach to empower individuals to unlock their true potential. Mona's unwavering commitment, expertise, and genuine care make her a guiding light for those seeking personal growth. Through her coaching and speaking engagements, she illuminates the path to success, fulfillment, and self-discovery for her clients.

Follow her on IG @Clearthegray_coaching

Take Your Life Back—You Only Get One

By Candace Holyfield–Parker

"Never let the fear of striking out keep you from playing the game."
Babe Ruth

Life sometimes makes us smile. Life sometimes makes us cry. In each experience, we are alive and breathing, giving us the control to smile or cry. I found myself in a deep black hole, depressed after earning over 5 million dollars. One immature business decision took my life that I worked so hard to build. I fired myself from a company that was mine. It was time to be a founder and no longer work in the business. This one decision ripped my company apart. I lost my life even though I was alive. After months of blaming others, crying, cursing and being angry, I decided enough was enough. The mental capacity and strength to rebuild was a very tall ladder, but that is what resilience is all about. I uncovered strategies to take my life back and maintain it.

Identify and Leverage Your Strengths

The journey to personal growth and success begins with recognizing and harnessing your strengths. Many of us possess abilities that can lead to remarkable achievements when identified and nurtured. In this transformative journey, recognize and actively cultivate your innate talents to impact the world. Seek roles that align with your strengths and values. Create a list of activities that bring you joy, make you lose track of time, or ignite you. These are strong indicators of your area of interest and potential strengths. Embrace challenges as opportunities to reveal your strengths and push you to grow. When faced with another roadblock, observe how you respond. Do you demonstrate resilience, adaptability, or the ability to think critically? These moments can highlight hidden strengths that you can cultivate and rely on in the future. You can take personality and strengths assessments on www.gullup.com. These tests help you better understand areas where you have comparative advantages.

Seek Professional Support

Recovering from any loss often requires professional support. Reach out to a licensed therapist. Therapy saved my life. It provides a safe space to explore the root cause of your coping mechanisms and learn valuable tools to navigate challenging emotions. Seeking help is a sign of strength and can significantly impact your recovery journey. Two professional resources: Dr Tina Pipkin @waistedbydrtina and LaTonia Taylor @rebithwithlatonia, both are their Instagram handles. Dr. Tina built me a prayer closet, which has been my safe haven and war room for the past seven months.

Practice Self Compassion

During recovery, it's essential to be kind and avoid self-criticism. Understand that healing takes time and that setbacks are a natural process. Treat yourself with the same compassion you would extend to a dear friend facing similar challenges.

Set Realistic Goals

Rebuilding your life may involve starting anew in various aspects. Set realistic and achievable goals for yourself, whether related to work, relationships, hobbies or personal growth. Break these goals into smaller manageable steps to avoid overwhelming yourself. Celebrate every milestone, no matter how small, as each one signifies progress on your journey.

Embrace Mindfulness and Wellness

Incorporate mindfulness practices into your daily routine to stay present and cultivate a positive mindset. Engage in activities that promote overall well-being such as mediation or pursuing creative outlets. Nurturing physical and emotional health can empower you to take control of your life and cultivate resilience.

Challenge Negative Thought Patterns

Depression or anxiety often creates a pattern of negative thinking. Work on identifying and challenging negative thought patterns. Practice reframing your thoughts into more positive and constructive perspectives. Remember that thoughts are not facts; you can change how you perceive and respond to them.

Taking back control of your life is a courageous, transformative journey. It requires patience, self-compassion, and willingness to seek help and embrace change. It's okay to take one step at a time. I am still taking steps to this day. Be gentle with yourself during setbacks. The right mindset and support, you reclaim your life and create a future filled with hope, purpose and fulfillment. Your resilience and strength will guide you toward a brighter, more empowered tomorrow.

Candace Holyfield–Parker

    Candace Holyfield–Parker, affectionately known as The Six Figure Spa Chick, is an international empowerment speaker, best-selling author, massage therapist with over 20 years of experience in the health/wellness industry, founder of Spa Boss Tribe (the largest black spa community in the world) and community service leader. She has devoted her life to supporting women and men to live the life they deserve. Twenty-three millionaires have been birthed from Candace's support, and her vision can be found in Essence, Entrepreneur, and Black Enterprise, to name a few. The city of Atlanta awarded Candace her very own appreciation day to applaud her community service work.

Powered By God: Bounce Back To Bounce Up

By Alexandria Evelyn Johnson

"I can do all things through Christ who strengthened me."
Philippians 4:13 KJV

Sir, for the Master of Science in Clinical Psychology, I present Alexandria Johnson. My victory was finally won. It took me six years to finally have my turn to walk across the podium to receive my degree. I graduated four years behind my cohort.

As a reward for my potential, my workplace granted me a two-year paid study leave. After completing my leave, I handed in a letter of academic probation. I was kicked out of university for repeatedly failing to pass an examination, so it seemed. I returned to work without celebration but with thick layers of shame. I survived the barrage of 'when' and 'what' questions. I survived being told that I was not focused while on leave. I survived being told I was too ambitious and must slow down my striving. I survived being told, 'You spent too much time praying and not studying.' I survived seeing people I respected and loved struggle to stand by me because I seemed to be a failure. My weight gain of nearly 100 lbs was narrating my story of pain, but the few who noticed asked, 'Why are you getting so big' and the others did not say a word. My friends accused me of 'acting up' but did not see that I was on psychological life support. I learned a few lessons from this experience and may these inspire your bounce back to bounce up.

Lesson One - Success is not always a bump-free ride.

This season of my life forced me to challenge everything that I knew about the success process. Success is much more than starting and finishing. Rather, it's more about growing through the difficulties of the journey. Swirling. Swooping. Swinging. Screaming. Shouting. Sighing. Hang On! Don't let go! When the ride stops, you will be at your destination. Don't look at someone else cruising down success highway; hold on to your wagon and watch the road. You, too, will arrive at your destination after a little adventure. Your story will be more interesting.

Lesson Two - Ask yourself, 'What About The Other Parts Of Me?'

You will always have one more fight left, no matter how difficult the battle is. When my graduate school journey became smeared with failure, I was lost in fear and shame. Fear and shame morphed me into a tattered and unrecognizable version of myself. Inspired by the Holy Spirit, after a time of prayer, I asked myself, what about the other parts of me? I drew a pie chart and reduced this whole experience to one slice of pie 'school'. I got to see that other parts of me were pulsating with life. I borrowed energy from the parts of me that were alive and resituated my self-esteem. I completed another master's degree program and then began a Ph.D. program while being kicked out of school. What else do you have in you?

Lesson Three - Celebrate The Journey

Bring out the whistles! Blow the confetti! It's time to celebrate in the middle of the mess. Celebration is a declaration that God is faithful and will turn every bad situation for our good. I was angry at my journey because I felt stagnated in my career. My anger was kryptonite. I also realized that I was blooming at the lowest point of my life. I became more patient, compassionate, driven, bold, and motivated to test my limits. As I began to magnify and intensify these traits, I slowly transformed into a radical force. Do you know we can never tap the deepest depths of our potential and strength until we are tried by fire? Celebrate the journey.

My name is Alexandria Johnson. I have Associate of Arts degrees in Psychology and Sociology; a Bachelor of Arts in Psychology; a Master Of Science in Clinical Psychology, a Master of Science in Child Forensic, and am a Ph.D. candidate. This is not a brag. This is evidence of my bounce back to bounce up. This is a testament to God's delivering power when my destiny was under siege. I fought to change my family's legacy from dropouts to graduates and reversed a vagabond culture where everyone's story ended with 'I almost did it.' You may wonder why your fight is so hard. Your genealogy is counting on you to bounce back to bounce up. You will survive it all. Take up your cross. Fight. God powers you.

Alexandria Evelyn Johnson

Alexandria Evelyn Johnson hails from The Bahamas. She is a Clinical Psychologist and Child Forensic Expert. She also completed specialized training in Mental Health Psychosocial Support Co-ordination, Addiction Treatment, and Youth Leadership. She is a certified Cognitive Behavioural Life Coach and a Christian Life Coach. For the past eleven years, she has served countless clients, helping them live optimally from the inside out.

She passionately serves in ministry and her community. She is an ordained Youth Pastor and Minister. For the past 15 years, she has been invited to speak nationally and internationally, promoting mental and spiritual wellness. She is a three-time best-selling author. She is the CEO at Winners Avenue Books and Salt and Light International. She instills hope through her work. Connect with her via email at winwithwinnersavenuebooks@gmail.com or saltandlightweare@gmail.com.

Footprints of Resilience: Leaving a Lasting Legacy

By Sherrie L. Johnson

"Like the transformation of a new butterfly,
keep going and never give up."
Sherrie L. Johnson

In the quiet hours of the night, I held my pregnant belly, anticipating hearing my daughter's heartbeat and seeing the outline of her image on the ultrasound at my weekly scheduled appointment. Little did I know that my world was about to shatter as I lay there on the examination table twenty-eight weeks into my pregnancy. The monitor was silent, and the image of her was still. The look on my doctor's face as she looked closely at the monitor was that of concern. She tried to reassure me with her words as she left the room to get my husband and the X-ray tech. The look on my husband's face told me she had a conversation with him before he entered the room.

The news of a stillbirth crushed me. I experienced several emotions: grief, sorrow, and anger. Nothing prepares you for the delivery of your child, knowing they will not be alive. After giving birth, I held her as long as possible because I knew I would never get to have her again once I let go. She looked so perfect. I thought to myself, "What went wrong?" I would give anything to see her chest rise and fall, anything for her to open her eyes. We had her cremated. That way, we could take her home with us. All I had left was the ink impression of her footprints.

In the days that followed my stillbirth, I was filled with anger, confusion, and overwhelming heartache. I wanted to scream. I couldn't cry out because my husband and son needed me to be strong. Even though my body had carried life, it felt empty and broken. Family members on both sides come in from out of town. No one wanted me to be alone. Feel alone. "Lord, why her? Why now?" During my first pregnancy, I was an unwed, unemployed, seventeen-year-old high-school senior sleeping on a foam mattress behind the door in my grandmother's one-bedroom apartment in the projects. I gave birth to my son in the county hospital all alone. This time, I am married, employed, and living in the suburbs. I began to question my faith in God. The weight of grief threatened to consume me. I couldn't do this alone. I joined a bereavement support group for women.

Amid sorrow, I discovered resilience did not mean the absence of pain but the willingness to embrace it. I allowed myself to grieve profoundly and unapologetically, understanding that my tears were a testament to my love for my stillborn child. After each meeting, I realized I was not alone in my journey. Sharing my story, opening up about my loss, and allowing others to witness my pain helped me. I found strength in vulnerability, knowing that through commonality and empathy, healing could flourish.

As the days turned into weeks, weeks turned into months, and months into years, I could celebrate my happiness as her mother. Some of my daily affirmations are "I give myself permission to grieve." "I release any and all self-judgment and embrace this journey." "I transform this grief into a tribute of love and remembrance." Eventually, I found the courage to give motherhood another chance. I gave birth to my son and then my daughter. Years later, I started a business, Jada Prints LLC, in honor of my daughter, Jada Simone Johnson. The colorful butterfly in the logo inspires hope for the future. It symbolizes my personal growth during this journey of loss and healing. As the CEO/Designer, each creation is made with a mother's love.

Sherrie L. Johnson

Sherrie L. Johnson is a dedicated mother of three children: Nickolaus, Kori, and Layla-Simone. After over two decades, she retired from a local law enforcement department in Virginia. Sherrie's passion for helping others is a testament to her character. She remains steadfast in her mission to empower others and is a beacon of hope for those seeking transformation.

Sherrie proudly served in the US Army. Sherrie is pursuing her master's degree in criminal justice from Virginia State University, where she is a Lifetime Member of the Chesterfield Alumni Chapter. When Sherrie L. Johnson is not making custom creations, she is out in the community, changing the mindset of the youth by providing proven strategies through entrepreneurship to change their current circumstances. A portion of every sale goes towards her community outreach initiatives. For more information, contact her at sherrie@jadaprints.com. Facebook;

Jada Prints LLC Instagram: @jadaprints Etsy: GiftsbyJadaPrints

Delayed But Not Denied

By Theresa Judge, MBA, MPA

"I know the plans I have for you," declares the Lord, "plans to prosper
you and not harm you, plans to give you hope and a future."
Jeremiah 29:11

I am a planner. I have never been a "let's just play it by ear" kind of person. I'm more of the type who likes to be in control of what's next on the agenda of my life. When I'm in control, I'm well prepared and I don't feel anxious about my future. So, what happens when a person who likes to be in control suddenly isn't? Chaos ensues and this chapter becomes a lot more interesting, or depressing, depending on your perspective.

While living in Virginia, I received a job offer for an exciting opportunity. The perks included a higher salary, working in a different industry, and relocating to another state. The timing couldn't be more perfect. I had been applying for a new job because I felt stuck in the management position I held at the time, as there was limited possibility for advancement. I knew it would be a major transition, but being the ambitious person that I am, I decided to accept the role anyway.

There I was, enjoying my new profession while residing near a thriving metropolitan area that I loved. There was always a concert, theatrical production, or special event happening to keep me occupied. Life. Was. Good. That is, until it wasn't. After only three years into my journey, I hit a bump in the road. I found out I was being laid off. Now, I was intimately familiar with downsizing as my previous positions in Human Resources and People Management entailed my involvement in at least three layoffs by this point in my career. However, I had never actually been on the chopping block myself. The pressure to quickly find a

43

replacement source of income was extremely stressful. I remember placing a post-it note on my computer monitor in my office notating the salary I wanted to be paid for my next position. That visual reminder served as motivation for me to identify my next BETTER opportunity. Unfortunately, after several months of job searching that BETTER opportunity never materialized. I eventually came to the realization that I had to move back to my previous home, and I wasn't referring to Virginia. I had grown up in South Carolina, cohabitating with my parents. After nearly a decade away, that is where I reluctantly returned.

For someone who had always been a great student, I felt like I had failed the test of life. I was a well-educated, articulate, talented, unemployed middle-aged woman who now had an 11:00 pm curfew (figuratively, not literally). To add insult to injury, my employment search wasn't progressing any better in the Palmetto state.

Cue the lightning because I was in the midst of a stormy season. A dear friend from Virginia and my best friend since childhood passed away within two years of each other. When I finally did get an interview for a great position, it was scheduled on the day of my childhood friend's funeral. I was giving remarks. Nevertheless, after the funeral I had a phone interview, and was immediately hired! It was a six-month assignment that got extended for close to a year. I prayed it would become permanent and was genuinely surprised when my supervisor delivered the news that my job was ending, AGAIN.

I felt my anxiety begin to take hold, but I refused to be defeated. I secured another temporary assignment within a few weeks. Shortly after I started, I was offered a permanent management position with the EXACT salary I wrote on the post-it note years before. This was the BETTER opportunity I prayed for. I believed it would happen. I had just arrived early for my blessings. That's what I surmise whenever life skews my plans but ultimately works out in God's perfect timing.

I recommend using the mantra, "Don't Worry, Be E.A.R.L.Y." whenever your plans go awry. It's a reminder to:

Embrace Change. Don't allow what you KNEW to be true in the past to deter you from discovering a NEW opportunity in the future.

Affirmations strengthen a positive mindset. Write down your affirmations and Scriptures. Say them aloud. Then place them in your line of sight for daily motivation.

Remind yourself of what you have already accomplished. Gratitude can sustain you when depression attempts to mentally detain you.

Learn to be patient. Have faith in God's favor over your life, for we know the plans God has for us. Therefore, don't be dismayed when your plans are delayed…

You just arrived early for your blessings.

Theresa Judge

Theresa Judge is a speaker, author, screenwriter, playwright, and poet. She is also the CEO of Next Level Creations, LLC, where she specializes in meeting and event planning services. Theresa's passion to collaborate with business leaders to design event experiences that educate, empower, and inspire the masses is unmatched. The writing creative recently released an affirmation journal titled "Mirror Talk: Reflect A Positive Image of Your Soul", which is currently available on Amazon.

Through her memberships in public service organizations including Delta Sigma Theta Sorority, Inc., Top Ladies of Distinction, Inc., and the National Association of University of Women, among others; Theresa has proven to be a visionary who is dedicated to giving back to the community. She possesses a Bachelor of Science in Integrated Marketing Communications from Winthrop University, an MBA in Human Resources Management from Webster University and an MPA in Public Leadership from Regent University.

Visit www.nextlevelcreationsllc.com.

When God Gives You the Vision, He also Gives You Provision

By Regina Kenan - Lady Lion'ness

"When you want to succeed as bad as you want to breathe, then you'll be successful."
Eric Thomas

I remember that day so clearly last summer while visiting my family in NC. My mentor told me that God had spoken to him and told him to call me immediately because he had a word for me. God said for me to go outside into my sister's backyard by myself because he needed to talk to me. So, I'm standing in my sister's backyard, and God says to me that I'm moving you back to NC because that is where your ministry will start, so go back to Buffalo and start packing and trust me. Ya'll let me tell you something that was one of the hardest things I have ever had to do in my life. No mother wants to hear that she has to move away and leave her babies. I debated with God because I did not want to leave my daughter and my grandkids. We had never lived apart, and I always wanted to be there for her to help her with her kids. God told me that you are hindering your daughter more than you're helping her, but your trust in me and the process is what I had to do.

When I returned to Buffalo, I unloaded my truck, went to Walmart, purchased boxes and bins, and did as my father told me to do. I had no idea how to break the news to my grandkids because we have such a close bond. I didn't want them to think I was abandoning them to go off and live my best life.

I said, " Lord, I do not have the money nor the help to move, and I don't see how I will be able to make this happen. My mentor quickly reminded me that in the bible, the book of Deuteronomy 31:8 says God will never leave you, nor will He forsake you, but He will be there with you always. When God gives you the vision, he will always give you the provision.

I cried every day for a month, not knowing what would happen to them if I wasn't there to protect my daughter and the kids, but God said I can protect them better than you can, so I need you to trust me. God always has a plan for us that we can't see through our own eyes. We must let go and let God have his way. I had to move out of God's way so that he could provide a better life for me and my daughter.

See, I never dreamed that my ministry would start in NC. I always thought it would be in Buffalo because I lived there. I had plans to start my ministry in Buffalo, but no matter what you have planned for your life, God always has something better for you. When you learn to trust the Lord with all your heart, you will see that God will provide your every need just like he said he would.

I lost some family members and friends because I chose myself for the first time. Who knew they would all turn their backs on me and make it look like I was trying to hurt my daughter and move away from her and my grandkids? I couldn't accept that my baby girl and I were not speaking, so I ended up canceling everything, but when God says move, you better move. I almost missed my blessing because I was letting the devil get the best of me, but when God has his hands in it, there is no way in hell the devil can win, no matter how hard he tries. So, when I started the journey, daggers were coming at me from every which way, but I did not let that stop me. I encourage you to put all your trust in the Lord and let him direct your path. My daughter and I's relationship is stronger than ever before. I am living in NC, returning to college, and getting my bachelor's degree in business administration at Fayetteville State University. There is nothing too hard for God. When God Gives You the Vision, He Also Gives You the Provision.

Regina Kenan

Regina Kenan is a motivational speaker, 4-time Amazon best-selling author, and the founder of Kenan Funeral Planning Services, Inc. Regina is a mentor and domestic violence advocate. She helps women transition from being a victim to becoming a victor and doing what God has called them to do.

Regina's passion is working with women and young girls by educating, empowering and encouraging them to build their self-esteem so they can walk into their calling and start their businesses. Regina is an Image Consultant; she helps women become more confident by looking great on the outside and feeling great on the inside so they can step and take their crown in the world.

Contact: ladylionnessden@gmail.com
Website: www.ladylionnessboutique.com
Instagram: Reginakenanladylionness

Don't Count Me Out, I Will Arise

By Marteka Landrum

"Even when walking through the dark valley of death I will not be afraid, for you are close beside me, guarding, guiding all the way."
Psalm 23:4

Violence was all around me in the early nineties. In September of 1993, it came to my front door when Daddy was murdered. Before this moment, I did not know how to identify emotions, take a stand, or fight. I did not learn these things from my family of origin. I desperately needed to know how to do them. After learning of his death, time stood still. As the youngest of six, having begun my senior year of high school, I had to make choices. I had to choose life or death. I had to choose to waste away or take responsibility for myself. I had to choose to suffocate under the weight of grief or learn how to communicate. I had to choose to run to God or run away from Him. I had to choose whether to forgive.

Oxford Languages defines resilient this way: "Able to recoil or spring back into shape after bending, stretching, or being compressed." There were many opportunities for me to be resilient. Even before I knew the word resilient, each opportunity was a choice for me to make. Before this moment in high school, I was unaware that my choice and voice had been taken away. It would take over twenty-five years for me to verbalize this.

One of my first decisions was knowing I would need God's help. I ran headlong into Him. I went mute, but I began journaling. Journaling was my way of release. I wrote daily. This is where I began to ask God all my questions and write about my day.

I also knew I had to learn how to communicate with others. Seeing a professional counselor helped me begin this process. Communication, specifically talking about emotions, was the beginning of bouncing back. This was a high-profile murder case with lots of rumors. Many times, it felt like everything was closing in on me. Sometimes, death seemed like a good idea. The pain of Daddy's death was intense—emotionally and physically.

I had decided to go to college. I went far away from Topeka, Kansas. I had to bounce back—be resilient—so I could leave the place that brought this pain. Away I went to Washington, DC, running from my problems. Soon, I had to seek resources to help me   remain resilient. I found a grief group that helped me spring back into shape after being compressed and stretched. I am thankful I spent two years at Howard University before the weight of my emotions and family dysfunction called for a timeout.

I returned to Topeka, started counseling again, and began exploring the thought that there's more of God to search out. I sprang back, but the shape was now different. It was different because I was different. The compression, bending, and stretching were causing me to take on a new shape while being resilient. Strength was arising from that compression, bending, and stretching. Searching for the more of God gave me things I didn't know I needed: resilience, energy, security, intuition, love, insight, eyes to see, a new voice and tenacity.

To be resilient, you must recognize you are not an island. We were created to operate in a community. We need each other for support. You need two to three sisters you can be real and raw with. You need a space to be your true, authentic self.

I began to find my voice. I began to realize that my voice mattered. I continued to make choices for life and choices that helped me spring back from being stretched or compressed. You can, too! Here's how:

- identify people who will hold you accountable to being your authentic self
- search for ways to deliberately nurture your spirituality
- writing (journaling) lets you get it out and later see your progress

- talking with a professional counselor/healer can help process roadblocks
- sharing your story helps you reflect on how you sprang back and also gives opportunities to see your progress

Your voice matters. Let us press on towards the high calling for which we have been called.

Resilience
Energizes the
Soul to
Ignite
Lessons that
Internalize
Embracing the
Next
Transformation

Resilient women arise!

Marteka Landrum

Marteka Landrum is a coach for teens experiencing trouble. She works with schools and parents by meeting teens where they are to help them take ownership of their experiences, help them better understand themselves, address their stress, and manage their motivations to build empowering relationships where conversations become peaceful, help form better bonds and foster success in and out of school.

Marteka enjoys helping others find their truth. She's a community builder who focuses on the individual working in various roles in education for over 20 years. Marteka's gift is her voice and ability to reach others with insight. Her purpose is to teach others how to be free. Through writing her first book, Broken Warrior: Be Empowered To Overcome, she hopes to let Christians know they can overcome past trauma, even after several years. Marteka is pursuing certification with the International Coaching Federation. Connect at www.positivechanges11.com.

Domestic Violence: Victim to Victorious

By Denise T. Mackey-Williams

"It's not just the bruises on the body that hurt.
It's the wounds on the heart and the scars on the mind."
Aisha Mirza

Domestic violence is a violent or aggressive behavior within the home that typically involves violent abuse of a spouse or a partner. According to the Department of Justice, "Domestic violence can be physical, sexual, emotional, economic, psychological, or technological actions that influence another person within an intimate partnership or relationship. This includes any behaviors that intimidate, humiliate, isolate, fight, terrorize, coerce, threat, blame, hurt, injure or wound someone."

I dated my ex-husband for two years, between 1983 and 1985. He was the perfect gentleman. We were so compatible and always had so much fun together. We got married in September of 1985 following our son's birth on May 31, 1985. A week after we got married, my husband changed. He began to accuse me of being unfaithful. Sometimes, I came home from work and didn't know whether I would get a kiss or a fist greeting me as I opened my front door. I worked at City College in New York and had to wear sunglasses to cover the bruises, cuts, and scars on my eyes and face. I was beaten so badly at times, that I could not get out of bed and was threatened not to call the police or hospital. There were nights I was awakened being punched in my face and thrown out of bed. One of my husband's favorite lines was, "You destitute black b_ _ _ _ _ from the projects." He called me so many awful names I started to believe

55

I was ugly. I was a victim of domestic violence. I felt sad and unhappy to live in this world. I suffered physical and mental abuse almost every day for three years until I couldn't take it anymore. Protecting my son's health and well-being also gave me the strength to leave my husband.

One day, I came home after work with a police officer, packed all my belongings, took my son and never looked back. Because of leaving my abusive husband, his revenge was when he hired five ladies to beat me down after leaving the entrance of the building where I worked at City College in Harlem, New York City. After being released from the hospital, I moved to the Bronx and pursued a teaching career. The devastation of this experience left me feeling depressed and unsure about the decisions I made for my life moving forward.

Today, I am happy to say that I am stronger, physically and mentally in control, doing well and on the road to prosperity. Today, I feel I am victorious and resilient! I had the power to get back up and dust myself off hard enough to be determined to make the best of my life.

If you've ever been a victim of domestic violence, here are important things to remember:

- You deserve a safe, happy life
- It is not your fault that you were battered and mistreated
- Like anyone else, you should be treated with respect

Remember that you are not in this world alone. Some resources to help you with domestic violence include:

1. The National Domestic Violence Hotline (1-800-799-7233).
2. The National Resource Center on Domestic Violence (1-800-537-2238).
3. The Strong Hearts Native Helpline (1-844-762-8483).

Denise T. Mackey-Williams

Ms. Denise T. Mackey-Williams is a motivational speaker who specializes in assisting individuals with time management. Denise earned a Bachelor's Degree in Liberal Arts and a Master's Degree in Substance Abuse Counseling. She works at Montgomery College in Maryland, has been an educator for thirty-five years, and received the "Board of Regents Staff Award" in 2018. She founded Coppin Student Parent Organization as an advisor and mentor at Coppin State University. Denise was a keynote speaker at the Winners Summit and an honoree of the prestigious EPSY Award for Excellence in Professional Speaking in June of 2023. She also co-authors the Number One Best Seller, "Get in The Game." Denise was also advertised as a professional speaker in the "Powerhouse Speakers Dominating 2023" magazine in July 2023. She believes the goal is not to waste time, but to use it effectively.

Echoes of Hope

By Maria Mbanga-Mazvimavi

"Weeping may endure for a night, but joy cometh in the morning."
Psalm 30:5

We are born and are given names; my mother was pregnant with me when my grandmother passed on. This invariably is how I became Maria Magdalena, but then there was the name Mother gave me unwittingly symbolized who I was to be in later years. Nosizi, the one with a big heart. As I grew up, I became everything my grandmother was, with all traits as I am told, but I believed I am truly my mother's daughter, and my mother was my biggest influence, she shaped the woman that I have become.

I went back drawn by what kept on ringing in my head. The line became my heading and beacon. It became the magnet that pulled to reality "When the flowers had dried, it became a poem in my head. It became me. It became my link to my mum. It is the reality that I tasted death and could not spit. It became my telescope into the high heavens. It became a chime and melancholy in my ear. It became the voice that said hush, hush, my dearest, everything is going to be alright, it became the lullaby, cry not my daughter. When the flowers dried, it came out as "usacheme" I will not leave you,"linda mntanami", I stared at the dry flowers and the mountain of earth it came "the greatest Psalmist 23Yea though I walk through the valley of the shadow of death, I will fear no evil : for thou art with me ;Thy rod and thy staff comfort me…"I had to trust the good book and the good lord for the pain I was feeling was piercing the very core of my soul and being. How was I going to cope? How was I going to face another day, another night? Mama, you told me to believe, to have faith, to never give up hope, for tomorrow will always be a better day. The storm raging in my soul, grief won't leave me alone, and the harsh whispers remind me not to weep and be still. Yes, Mum, I hear you, the butterfly flies past. I walked away, aware the flowers had dried withered; an earth battered by rains. There was the shrub we grew on that, and I knew there was hope from a child.

I could hear my mother's voice clearly say, don't cry for me, for mine is a journey travelled to full breath, a fight taken to a hilt and a spiritual journey ready to be with my maker and ready to have one more dance with my beloved husband.

My fight with cancer was my path our dear lord chose to transition to heaven. Nosizi, she would whisper, lion princess, a lot is expected out of you, but understand the vitals first, perseverance, persistence, and excellence. Do us proud, be our Madikizela. Be our Condoleezza Rice. Be our Hillary Clinton, be our Ellen Johnson Sirleaf. Be our Mother Theresa. Be Us first and foremost. Should there be challenges in life, I left some cows in Insiza. They are your security and buffer to finishing what may seem impossible. Focus and always keep your eyes on the ball.

I will not be there to see you become the firebrand advocate, don't worry, daughter love, I will look to see you up from heaven pacing those streets and high offices, fighting for the dignity of every girl child and woman. I will see you score victory after victory. I remember the day you rebuked a man who had abused a girl child. Fearless and bold at only sixteen. I knew you were cut out to be a trailblazer and change agent. The young girl, not-so-young small-town girl, has become the "policewoman" of law and order and human rights. I smiled with satisfaction as that was a precursor to what would come. Love for what you do, love and compassion for humanity and mankind will see you through and remain authentic and true. You are an original. There is one you and no carbon copy. Remember "Ubuntu" "I am because we are "and no matter how far you travel, never forget the green grass of home, never forget your roots. Lastly don't be harsh on self, love, forgive and pray. God is always faithful and on time. He will not give what you cannot handle.

Maria Mbanga-Mazvimavi

Maria Mbanga-Mazvimavi is a Women and Girl Child Empowerment Advocate, Community Builder, Leader, Philanthropist and Motivational Speaker. She is the Founder of Woman and Hope for Her Global and a Published Author. She has a podcast called Sisters Talk, Up Close and Personal with Maria, where she interviews women from around the globe who advocate for women and girls' issues varying from education, law and justice and women's advancement. An English Literature teacher and Banker by profession. After graduation, she sought to serve in the most disadvantaged communities in the peri-urban around the globe. Maria believes. education is the door to freedom, offering a chance for a brighter future. I am a true disciple of home is best I believe my God willing; I am a better citizen alive, and tomorrow will be able to help rebuild a better community for the children who are the future.

The Real Snapback: Reclaiming the ME in MOMmy

By Carol T. Muleta

"Restore all that was hers, together with all the produce of the fields from the day that she left the land until now."
2 Kings 8:6

A snapback, defined as a "sudden rebound or recovery," can apply to business/finance, sports, and even relationships. The term is also used by and about mothers regarding their ability to 'snap back' into physical shape after giving birth, almost as if the event never happened. Mothers are often celebrated for the speed of their snapback. Regardless of a mom's outward appearance, I'm not sure a snapback is a desirable or realistic outcome. After all, why embark on such a spectacular journey only to return unchanged by it?

Indeed, welcoming a child should usher in transformation and not a rush to revisitation, particularly on the inside. After giving birth to my twin sons, I realized that parenting carries a lot of weight that is not so easily shed, outside or especially inside. I felt the very real weight of responsibility – "These boys will depend on me in many ways for a long time." I couldn't ignore the weight of fear and worry – "I'm sure I'll make mistakes along the way." Finally, I had to consider the weight of hope and expectation – "I want my sons to grow up to be smart/kind/ happy/successful… "and the list went on.

Children demand and deserve a huge share of our bandwidth in some seasons more than others. That's a fact but not a terminal truth. Thankfully, I understood that, but caring for two infants at once was exhausting early on. Down the road, as my children become more active, outspoken and independent, I actually pined for the good old days when they hung on my every word and hardly left my side. All the while, though, the 'weight' of motherhood was shifting. Over time, it began to fall away, though never completely.

My evolving motherhood experience has taught me a few things. First, be intentional about the weight you want to release. Hold on to too much, and you won't be able to soar into your next chapter. Release too much, and you lose the enrichment and hard-earned enlightenment you gained on the journey. I invite you to consider these transformative questions whose answers will position you to reclaim the ME in MOMmy. They did for me.

What's important now? Identify your guiding values and priorities as you parent. My mission to prepare my toddler son for life became urgent when he was diagnosed with developmental delays. As the Cheshire Cat told Alice in Wonderland, "If you don't know where you're going, any road will take you there." Clarity illuminates your choices.

What's the plan? Identify the values you uphold and design the routines and practices that best honor them. Firm principles will hold you steady when factors like judgment by others or unforeseen circumstances threaten to distract or derail you. Life won't always unfold as   expected, but a plan equips you to pivot purposefully.

What do you have in the house? Like the widow whom Elisha questioned in 2 Kings 4:2, you must take inventory of what you possess that could help you meet the moment. Material assets, life experiences, or insights you've acquired are resources that can and should be leveraged in this season. Don't underestimate the value of what you can bring to parenting or any role, even if it seems meaningless, like the small jar of oil the widow initially discounted.

What do you need? You can't be prepared for everything, so be honest about what you lack and figure out how to get it. If someone else has it, ask for it. If it requires new skills, become a humble student. If it doesn't exist yet, create it. Respect yourself enough to set yourself up for success.

What have you decided? Nigerian Beauty mogul Tara Fela Duratoye says, "Life never gives you what you deserve, but what you decided." As a mother AND woman, you can be as courageous, caring, and impactful as you make up your mind to be. Decide you will bring your best self to the table, then serve up your brilliance.

If that matters to you, an aesthetic snapback is nice, but it shouldn't be your primary aim. Strive to emerge from the most intense and powerful seasons of parenting in a way that reclaims your authentic human identity and embraces the enlightened evolution you've been experiencing. My motherhood journey birthed my passion for empowering kids and families and launched me in a new direction, professionally. Thankfully, I'm still ME, only better!

Carol T. Muleta

Carol T. Muleta is a Parenting Strategist and Consultant. She oversees The Parenting 411®, a resource hub where she delivers "information parents need from sources they can trust." Carol empowers parents to find JOY in their journey, using her fresh approach to discipline, communication, and family connection. Carol reaches parents through keynotes, webinars, coaching, and The Parenting 411® Podcast. She was named 2019 District of Columbia Mother of the Year® by American Mothers, Inc. As host of the Parenting 411 radio show on Baltimore's Radio One talk radio station, she was named Radio Personality of the Year at SpeakerCon 2019. She is a 6x best-selling author whose most recent book was recognized as a finalist at the 2022 International Book Awards. Her signature talk, "Scaling Up: From Marketing Manager to Mother of the Year," has inspired many. Carol is the proud mom of twin sons who are now thriving young adults.

Trauma Created an Exodus: Now My Light Shines Bright

By Dr. Emma Norfleet

"Trauma creates change you don't choose. Healing is about creating change you do choose."
Michele Rosenthal

Did you know statistically that the number one cause of "death" for the age group 1 – 46 is "TRAUMA? My, my, what an alarming statistic. However, after sharing my story, I'm sure you will agree God's Grace, Mercy, and Favor kept me from being a part of this age group. Trauma is a deeply disturbing, distressing, and life-threatening situation or circumstance that includes the following: physical, emotional, sexual, and environmental dangers that the trauma victim can directly or indirectly experience. Both direct and indirect trauma can cause immediate and lifetime mental health concerns. The most common mental health concerns are post-traumatic stress disorder, major depression, generalized anxiety disorder and substance use/abuse. Post-traumatic stress disorder, major depression, generalized anxiety disorder, and substance abuse. For many people, trauma takes them to a very dark and helpless space. As early as age 5, I could have been in the above statistic.

Many know that Askmsemma, the Trauma Expert/this writer, was dragged through the woods by her brother after a drunken father shot at them. You're probably wondering why my brother dragged me into the woods. Well, this brother had disrupted a drunken father's attempt to rape their older sister, which enraged the father so much he tried to kill my brother. In the father's inebriated state, he discharged the weapon after the brother and other siblings sought safety in the woods. However, God's Grace, Mercy, and Favor prevailed because no one died.

The early trauma at age five was dark, but the darkness of trauma wasn't finished with me. God's Grace, Mercy, and Favor saved me from three car accidents, but with each accident, I walked away unharmed. And all three car accidents fell within the age group (1 – 46), whereby trauma is known to be the number one cause of death. I've shared both direct and indirect trauma, but the most horrific direct trauma was my heart attack on November 27, 2021, the last day of an Aruba vacation. Adding insult to injury, the trauma of a heart attack was further complicated by the hospital in Aruba lacking the technology to do the surgery required to SAVE MY LIFE. Then I was rushed back to the U.S. to undergo open heart surgery.

And yes, again, God's Grace, Mercy, and Favor prevailed. I stand strong today, sharing this Exodus story with you. Now, hold on to your seat because, despite the physical trauma my body had endured, an unexpected direct emotional trauma, the ending of my marriage, amidst this major medical crisis occurred. So, what do you do when your life suddenly takes a sharp turn you never expected? The man who was supposed to love me forever checked out, and there I was left alone. However, shortly after that, I realized I needed this quiet and alone time to understand my divine assignment. Full circle, my light shines bright as I help survivors of trauma   TRIUMPH OVER TRAUMA because MY WELLNESS FOR SELF IS NOW FOR SOMEBODY ELSE.

In conclusion and during the writing of this chapter, my Pastor (Rev. Patrick Walker) had   been preaching sermons about "The Life Lessons of Moses" from the book of Exodus. When God allows you to survive trauma, as did both Moses and I/Askmsemma, not only was it a blessing, but evidence of being RESILIENT and resolved to the WHY without knowing how. I leave these golden nuggets to help you navigate, manage and cope with trauma if you're in a dark and hopeless space.

1. Through all the trauma I survived, God's Grace, Mercy, and Favor prevailed; therefore, if you trust God and his divine path for your Exodus, you will prevail.

2. When trauma comes and takes you to a dark space, REFLECT on your divine purpose for others after surviving trauma: and then REJECT the enemy's trick that you can do this on your own, and RESET your mind to the fact that God's Grace, Mercy, and Favor in your bright life could be light for others' dark space.

3. Then ask yourself, "Am I living my blessed and best life?" If the answer is No, use the next golden nugget to further your resiliency.

4. Schedule an intake for one of 4 outpatient evidence-based psychotherapies: Cognitive Processing (CP); Eye Movement Desensitization Reprocessing (EDMR); Prolonged Emotive (PE) and Trauma-Focused Cognitive Behavioral (TF-CBT) therapies.

I pray this chapter will create your Exodus if you have unresolved trauma.

Dr. Emma Norfleet

Dr. Emma Norfleet, PsyD., LCSW, LICSW, LCSW-C, CAMS I is the President/CEO of Haley's Mind of Services, LLC. She is a Psychotherapist, International Motivational Speaker, Author, and Amazon's #1 best seller in 4 coauthored book anthologies with Dr. Cheryl Wood & Les Brown. Authored/Released "How to Unmask and Resolve Trauma," in February/2022. HMOCS, LLC provides evidenced-based psychotherapies that help clients "TRIUMPH OVER TRAUMA." Emma facilitates CEU training for clinicians needing licensure. Her MISSION is to help thousands of SURVIVORS OF TRAUMA learn how to "TRIUMPH OVER TRAUMA."

Contact Info:
Website www.hmocs.org.
Work number: (240)429-5390 & email: info@hmocs.org.
Instagram: @askmsemma & facebook.com/emma.norfleethaley.

C^4 = A Resilient You!

(Core Values, Curiosity, Courage, Commitment)
By Adalena Oliver

"You may encounter many defeats, but you must not be defeated. In fact, it may be necessary to encounter the defeats, so you can know who you are, what you can rise from, how you can still come out of it."
Maya Angelou

Core values are fundamental beliefs and guiding principles that shape our behavior, decisions, and actions. I consider them the most essential things in our lives and reflect our sense of identity, purpose, and priorities. When we recognize and embrace our core values, they act as an emotional shield of armor that makes us resilient and lets us navigate through difficult times with strength and grace. Core values, curiosity, courage, and commitment are the key ingredients to building A Resilient You! If it were not for these qualities, I would not be here to tell my story today.

I grew up in Chicago and come from a huge family. I'm number 10 of 11 children. My dad and mom, both deceased, were married for 53 years before my mom passed away. My dad worked his entire life to provide for us. My mom stayed home to raise us. She never finished HS but eventually returned to school at 50 to get her GED. I remember thinking, how in the world did they do that? How did they stay married for 53 years? How did they love and raise 11 children? How did they ensure that we would get an education and become productive members of society? How did they keep us healthy, safe, and secure? And finally, how did they give each of us what we needed with leftovers for grandchildren and great-grandchildren? Amazing! We were not financially rich. Nor were we poor. While growing up, I always felt I had everything I needed and most of what I wanted. I was happy. Life was difficult, but it sure was good!

When I began writing my chapter for this book, the answer was revealed. My parents successfully loved, raised, and provided for 11 children because they were RESILIENT. I grew up watching examples of resilience play out right in front of my eyes every day. However, I did not know what I was looking at until now. A person's core values can easily be identified by observing where they spend their time and money. When I applied this concept to my parents, their values became crystal clear. They valued - family, commitment, hard work, education, and financial security. And guess what, so do I. However, my definitions differ from those of my parents. I have defined my core values based on my life experiences. And so does everyone, even if they don't know it!

Taking the time to identify your core values is the most critical step to becoming A Resilient You. You must complete this step for the formula to be effective. Collectively, core values, curiosity, courage, and commitment contribute to building your resilience in these ways:

• Core Values: Having well-defined core values gives you a sense of purpose and a moral compass. When faced with adversity, they provide a solid foundation that can help you stay true to yourself and maintain your integrity when dealing with challenges.

• Curiosity: Curiosity encourages you to approach difficult situations with an open mind and a willingness to learn. This growth mindset lets you view defeats as opportunities for growth and exploration rather than insurmountable obstacles.

• Courage: Courage enables you to confront fear and act despite uncertainty. With courage, you are more likely to step outside your comfort zone, embrace challenges, and persevere to build your capacity to handle anything.

• Commitment: Commitment involves being dedicated to your goals and willingness to stay the course, even when faced with obstacles.

Committing to completing your goals makes you more likely to endure difficulties and setbacks, as they fuel a strong sense of purpose.

When you combine the above four elements, over time, they form a strong foundation for A Resilient You! When faced with setbacks, with these attributes, you can draw on your values for guidance, maintain curiosity to find new solutions, summon the courage to overcome obstacles and show commitment to persevere and adapt. The synergy between core values, curiosity, courage, and commitment provides individuals with a holistic toolkit for building and sustaining a resilient life.\

Adalena Oliver

Adalena is a professional life and career coach, best-selling author and global speaker dedicated to helping her clients live a fulfilling, value-based life! She uses her 7-step process to help them identify their core values and use them as the foundation for getting their dream job and realizing their goals.

Adalena has an extensive career in corporate America. She mentors and coaches stakeholders at all levels to ensure that changes are embraced and successfully integrated to sustain long-term personal and organizational transformation. She is a life learner and views the world as her classroom.

Adalena Ahmad holds a BS in Sociology, an MS in Organizational Leadership, an MS in The Management of Information Technology, and several certifications, including Project Management, Change Management, and Coaching. In the spring of 2023, she received the Excellence in Professional Speaking Award from the National Academy of Professional Speakers, Authors and Coaches and an affiliate of The Global Speakers University.

Adalena Oliver, President and CEO of APMC, LLC
Leader, Mentor, Coach, Author, and Global Speaker

From Heartbreak to Healing

A Testament to Faith, Resilience, and the Transformative.

By Dr. Rita Reneé

"A happy life is the perfect life to which we are led by a firm faith,
cheerful hope, and fervent love."
Monica of Tagaste (c.331–387)

In a world often filled with heartbreak and shattered dreams, Dr. Rita Reneé's extraordinary story stands as a beacon of hope, illuminating the path of healing and self-discovery. After enduring a painful 16-year marriage marred by infidelity, Dr. Reneé found the strength to break free from the chains of betrayal and embark on a transformative journey that would redefine her worth and restore her faith in love.

The first year of her marriage, she has marked the beginning of Dr. Reneé's heartbreaking journey. She discovered that her husband had cheated on her, and the painful truth deepened when she learned that the other woman had become pregnant not once but twice, ultimately undergoing abortions. In a remarkable act of grace, Dr. Reneé found the strength within herself to pray with the woman who had become entangled in her marital turmoil. Her actions exemplified the power of forgiveness, compassion, and a resolute belief in the transformative nature of faith.

But the challenges did not end there. Time and time again, Dr. Reneé's husband continued to engage in affairs, leaving a trail of pain and broken trust in his wake. Women would contact her, sharing the devastating news of his infidelity. The weight of these betrayals plunged Dr. Reneé into a deep depression, and she grappled with suicidal thoughts. Despite urging her church and family to stay in the marriage for material reasons, Dr. Reneé made a life-altering decision: she chose to prioritize herself worth.

In Reneé this pivotal moment of self-realization, God revealed His boundless love and showed Dr. Reneé her true worth. With unwavering faith, she courageously left her past behind and started anew. Moving from Georgia, she embraced a fresh beginning, shedding the heavy burdens of shame and guilt that had weighed her down for far too long.

As Dr. Reneé embarked on her healing journey, she discovered that God had been working behind the scenes, orchestrating events for her ultimate good. When the divorce proceedings finally concluded in her favor, it was a moment of vindication. The shackles of shame and guilt were shattered, replaced by a profound sense of liberation and empowerment. Dr. Reneé's story serves as a potent reminder that, ultimately, our pain can pave the way for growth and transformation.

Amid her newfound freedom, God graced Dr. Reneé's life with the presence of a fantastic man who recognized and cherished her true worth. It was a testament to the redemptive power of love and the belief that, despite the trials we face, brighter days lie ahead.

Dr. Rita Reneé's journey offers valuable lessons for women who have experienced similar hardships. Her story reminds us of forgiveness, resilience, and embracing our inherent worth. Here are some viable steps and takeaways from her experience:

Embrace forgiveness and compassion: In the face of betrayal, choosing forgiveness can bring healing and freedom.

Seek support from a supportive community: Surround yourself with people who uplift and support you during challenging times. Lean on their strength and encouragement.

Rediscover your self-worth: Remember that the actions or opinions of others do not define your value. You deserve love, respect, and happiness.

Trust in divine timing: Have faith that everything happens for a reason, even when the present seems unbearable. Trust that God's plan for you is more significant than anything you can imagine.

Embrace new beginnings: Let go of the pain of the past and embrace the opportunities that lie ahead. Your journey toward healing and self-discovery begins with a courageous step forward.

Dr. Rita Reneé's story is a testament to the resilience of the human spirit and the transformative power of faith, forgiveness, and self-love. As she emerged from the depths of heartbreak, she found her true worth and love that honored and cherished her. May her journey inspire women everywhere to hold their heads high, knowing they deserve love, respect, and a future filled with hope.

Dr. Rita Reneé

Dr. Rita Reneé is the co-owner of Gibson and Gibson Licensed Financial Professionals, LLC, in Raleigh, NC. She is enthusiastic about providing financial literacy to help families and businesses save on taxes, build and protect their wealth, leave a legacy and not a liability, and create generational wealth.

In 2023, Dr. Rita Reneé founded Radiant Diamonds, which uses
executive business development, which builds, empowers, and uplifts women entrepreneurs to scale their businesses locally and globally. Her sole purpose is to be an obedient servant of God! "I want to be transparent with my testimony to help those to know the true power of God!" ... Without any Apologies!

Her promise verse: Philippians 1:6 For I am confident that He who began a good work in you will perfect it until the day of Christ Jesus.

Contact information: 919-390-0314
info@drritarenee.com
www.drritarenee.com
https://www.linkedin.com/in/drritarenee/
https://www.facebook.com/DrRitaRenee/

Resilience & Grief

By Coach Shar Robinson

"I no longer live but Christ lives in me."
Galatians 2:20

In 2009, I lost my very best friend and Ministry Partner to Breast Cancer, Missionary Karen Amuneke. When she died, I died! Losing her devastated my whole soul. After 10 years of suffering in silence, I realized, I was angry at God. I felt like God punked me because I fasted and prayed for her to live and she died. I watched the nurse pull the plug. Karen didn't pass immediately. I was hoping she would breathe on her own, and she was breathing on her own. Then, maybe a minute later, she flat-lined. With my last glimmer of hope, I felt punked again by God. I couldn't believe, with all the faith I had, Karen was dead.

The last words I heard my friend say were, "This is not unto death." I believed her. I had more than mustard seed faith, I had mountain seed faith. I'll never forget my kid's grandmother coming to ICU, and she told me afterward that she knew Karen was passing because her feet didn't look like they were getting oxygen. She said she couldn't tell me. I would not have been able to handle it. I was anointing her feet and in another World, very hopeful in my mind. Granny Deborah felt sorrow for me because she knew what death looked like, and I wasn't ready to accept it.

The lesson I learned was there are 2 sides of faith. She said, "You had faith to believe she would live. You didn't consider the other side of faith-what if she didn't live?" She was saying God is good whether Karen lives or not.

Granny Deborah's words helped me when I started healing and reconnecting my relationship back to God. I realized my friend left this

Earth in faith, and if I wanted to see her again, I would have to leave in faith, too, and it gave me the motivation I needed to pursue my purpose.

Depression looks different for everybody. I didn't know I was depressed. I was a workaholic, and I was not walking by faith. I was going to Church, not feeling anything, going to Church out of ritual, not relationship. I was unhappy and living a victim's life instead of a victor's life. I was drinking, hiding bottles under my bed; I collected and hid them but always marveled at how beautiful the bottles were. I was a functional alcoholic. I felt like I was addicted to grief. I was a "killjoy," and I isolated myself, and I never returned to Ministry until 14 years later in 2023. Grief took me out of the Church and into a state of "why have faith it doesn't work?"

How did I pick myself back up? I started realizing my friend would be disappointed if she knew I was not a Soul Winner.

We had this book called "Soul Winning." We loved that book. It read, "God's greatest commodity is souls." We were happy to call ourselves "Soul Winners." We had contagious faith and I wanted to love, trust God and feel again.

Here are 6 Tips to Help You Create Space to Receive More Joy After Loss:

1. Grieve Intentionally – The opposite of grief is joy. Create "happiness triggers that support you in pivoting from sadness. For example:
    A. Schedule a Day-Vay or Stay-cation (Road Trips, Resorts, Fun)
    B. Lit Candles
    C. Hiking or Walking
    D. Playing Cards
    E. Coloring Book or Crossword Puzzle

The point is, do not stay stuck. Continue to feel healthy feelings.

2. Create Daily Intentions–I intend to be productive and feel my feelings, so I experience fulfillment, fun, laughter, joy and peace.
3. Journal–Give your pain a voice.

4. Consider Hiring a Grief Coach–They will help you deal with what's happening.
5. Recognize Choice is Your Power–Make choices from a place of purpose, not trauma and fear.
6. Wake up Grateful–Wake up with a smile on your face for about 30 seconds and repeat if necessary. It can change the way you feel every day. Pray and praise before you get out the bed. Create a "gratefulness journal" for 21 days and watch yourself "shift."

I realized a few things:
1. The safest place in the World is in the Will of God.
2. The life I live is not my own.
3. God is living in me, working through me, as me.
4. Jesus died because of what He left in me to share with the world & build up His Kingdom.
5. Not living would not stop me from dying.

Coach Shar Robinson

Coach Shar is experiencing "new life" after being delivered from 10 years of depression, grief and sadness 2009-2019. She studied under Rev. Dr. Iyanla Vanzant's "Healing & Life Coach School" in Maryland for two years. She healed, reinvented her life and created an academy that lets hurting women heal in community. Through "Begin Again Academy," she offers her clients a safe place to heal, be heard, peel back layers of pain, face it and heal it. One of her signature healing activities is a "Trauma Time Line."

It lets clients connect to their root issues, patterns and customized solutions. She teaches 40 Kingdom Principles in 40 Days and supports clients in understanding their Subconscious Mind and God-Conscious Mind. Her motto is, "If you can feel it, I can help you heal it."

www.lifecoachshar.com.

Beyond Yesterday's Shadows Empowering Lives Through Our Troubled Pasts

By Kimberly Seabrooks

"Yesterday is not ours to recover, but tomorrow is ours to win or to lose."
Lydon B. Johnson

Sometimes, life can feel unfair. You could find yourself in a situation and wonder how you got there. You might even start questioning your existence, lose hope, and wish the universe were less cruel.

But amidst everything going on in your life, I am here to give you hope; I assure you that with time, everything will be okay, and at the end of it all, everything works out for the best.

Let me give you a short version of my life story.

Some years ago, I was born, but unfortunately, I didn't have the best parents anyone could wish for; they were both alcoholics, and my mother was diagnosed with bipolar disease. They used to call it manic depression then. So, from the day I was born, I was introduced to a chaotic environment - you can imagine how that is for a newborn. Due to all the drama and issues in the house, my parents had to let my grandmother take care of me.

Can you guess how old I was? Two weeks old.

I am guessing she was trying to help because she had other young children under her care, two of whom were sick.

This left me under the care of my 13-year-old aunt. As she tried her best to raise me, a family member took advantage of the vulnerability and molested me. No, they didn't do it once or twice; they kept abusing me from when I was 5 to 12 years.

This experience greatly affected my mental and emotional life. For the longest I can remember, I was a mess. The hurt and shame from that awful experience lingered until they became a part of me. It felt like anyone could read the whole story by looking at me. At some point, I felt like it was my fault. I didn't have the tools to understand that I didn't deserve all that happened, that I was a victim. Instead, I kept the story to myself and carried it like a badge of honor. Honestly, I was proud of it at some point. It was the reason I was broken, and since I thought I was the only person going through this, I made it a big part of my life.

My story isn't the best, and probably yours too, but I want you to know that you are not alone and there is hope.

You might wonder how I moved from being the broken child I was to the optimistic person I am today. Well, let me tell you of the day my life changed for the better.

One day, I opened up to my favorite aunt, who was a minister. During the conversation, she opened up to me too and told me she, too, was molested and shared her journey to healing from the dreadful experience she had.

This was my turning point. I, for one, realized that I was not crazy and was not the only person with a tainted past. Looking at how good she was doing and learning there are ways to deal with whatever life throws at us, I understood that my past didn't have to determine my future. I realized that I was no longer that scared kid who had the worst childhood and used my aunt's revelation to motivate me and work on myself for the sake of my tomorrow.

I share my story as a testament of resilience and hope, hoping it resonates with anyone with traumatizing past. No matter how ugly your story is, it doesn't have to define you; there is hope. You must learn how to divorce it because it is the only thing stopping you from having the life you wish. Sure, it is difficult to break free from the chains of our past, but with determination, patience, hope, and resilience, you can do it.

Together, let's rise above our misfortunes and empower each other to claim control of our lives. Embrace the power of hope to heal you, and once you do, use your past as a blessing to encourage and inspire others. Not as an albatross around your neck that will destroy your future. Let others know they, too, can and must learn to grow past their experiences to develop new ways of thinking for a better life.

Kimberly Seabrooks

Kimberly Seabrooks is a Certified Health Coach and a passionate advocate dedicated to empowering women to live their healthiest lives. As the founder of Kim's Health Coaching, a popular YouTube channel, Kimberly has built a strong online community where she shares practical health tips, advice, and inspiring stories. Her content resonates particularly with women in their 40s and 50s, addressing their unique dietary needs during this stage of life.

With a Bachelor's Degree in Business and close to half a decade in the field, Kimberly has dedicated herself to helping women navigate the challenges of aging with grace and vitality. Kimberly's specialization lies in coaching women going through menopause, offering valuable insights and strategies tailored to their unique needs. She emphasizes the importance of adjusting dietary habits to support hormonal changes and maintain ideal health as women age. Through her health coaching program, Kimberly has positively affected the lives of many women, helping them achieve deep physical and mental well-being.

Truth is Melatonin for the Soul

By Dr. Timogi

"Truth isn't always beauty, but the hunger for it is."
Nadine Gordimer

I'm a product of the incarcerating ideology of the "what happens in this house stays in this house" generation.

In the seventies, domestic violence was yet to be commonly recognized by doctors, the law, or psychologists. There were no cellphones to document in real-time, no Google to search for resources, and phone bills listed every call, including the number, time, and duration of each call so there was no discretion in seeking help. When researchers started to collect statistics on domestic violence in the late seventies, they took the position of the woman as a provocateur. There were no agencies to help my mother.

My mother's story is hers to tell, but as a child, watching her suffer was devastating. But additionally, it was the lying about my father's violence that sickened me almost as much as his brutality. We collectively lied by lying, silence, omission, and mostly by showing up as a perfect middle-class family. That was proven when I learned via Facebook from a middle school friend they called us "The Cosbys."

I was warned young to never speak of his womanizing and violence. If I did, I would be severely punished, which would be deemed my mother's fault, so she would be punished more. If he's not he wasn't afraid to do it, why should we have been afraid to say it? Ironically, my father hated a liar more than a thief! He told me as a little girl, I could lie to anyone, even my mother, just not to him. He demanded the Truth from everyone while his life was a lie. The Truth was so important to him he would beat it out of you until you told him what he wanted to hear.

We all live our Truth. If your life is a lie and that is what you're living, then your Truth is you're a liar. Speaking our Truth and owning our Truth is where we struggle.

I speak my Truth to my detriment at times. My Truth about the abuse and eventually being disowned by my father until his death because he couldn't control me. My Truth about the innumerable mistakes I have made in my life. Yes, people have used it against me. However, The the alternative for me is greater. The alternative is me suffering daily for what will one day be exposed. The alternative is hiding what needs to be healed, covering what needs to be corrected, and shielding what needs to be stopped! The alternative is letting the lie live and endorsing it in any capacity consciously or subconsciously.

The alternative is me bearing the mental, physical, and emotional burden of the offender, even when it's me. I'm not Jesus.

During my late thirties, in a miserable marriage and two small children, this stay-at-home mom with no resources needed help to leave. In my Truth, God led me to who would become my best friend, a psychotherapist, a principal who helped me at the children's school, and the additional resources I needed to create the life I desired. And, my mother's home who was finally away from her abuser.

When compelled to lie, especially about someone's behavior toward us, it is not for discretion or privacy as the stay-in-this-house adage implies. It's protection of our ego, which believes, "I am too smart, attractive, anointed, talented, and educated to be neglected, rejected, used, or abused." The ego does not want to be judged. However, in blocking judgment, the ego certainly blocks so much more.

There is safety in Truth. The "slippery when wet" sign tells the Truth about that surface so you can take the necessary precautions to pass over safely and reach your goal!

There is help in Truth. If you tell me you have a flat, but your battery is dead, a spare tire won't help. Truth will get you jump-started and on your way!

There is power in Truth. Lies deplete power. Truth unlocks the strength you need to create the life you want.

There is peace in Truth. Speaking your Truth means you don't go to bed every night wondering if tomorrow is the day you'll be exposed. Truth is melatonin for the soul.

Your capacity to endure, to recover from difficulties, to be resilient begins with Truth. Speak your Truth because you're already living it.

Dr. Timogi

Dr. Timogi is THE Empowerment Specialist helping individuals and organizations move from Elusive to Empowered. Her company Create & Facilitate, LLC brings customized training solutions to municipalities, corporations, non-profits, and universities. As a keynote speaker, Dr. Timogi has graced stages from prisons to Harvard. She has authored 12 books and writing her How to Write Your First Book course on Thinkific gives people the tool to tell their story. Dr. Timogi is a Professor and Pastor who lives in North Carolina but was raised out in Brooklyn.

Finding the Resilience Within

By Janet Tonkins

*"Do not judge me by my success, judge me by how many times I fell
down and got back up again!"*
Nelson Mandela

Resilience is the power to rise,
When life knocks us down with or without surprise.
It's the strength to keep moving on,
Even when the road ahead seems long.

Resilience is the courage to face,
The challenges that come our way with grace.
It's the determination to never give up,
And to keep pushing forward, no matter what.

Resilience is the hope that we hold,
When everything around us seems cold.
It's the faith that we have in God and ourselves,
To overcome any obstacle and excel.

Resilience is the light that shines,
When we're lost in the darkness of our minds. It's the fire that burns
within our soul,
To help us achieve our ultimate goal.

This is the story of a real estate mogul, Janet Tonkins, "The Cashflow
Diva, who buys houses like women buy shoes." She started in poverty,

living in the CCP projects of New Jersey, where violence, drug abuse, and low or no self-esteem were the norm. God knows she has had to be resilient to survive and be the architect of her environment instead of the victim. She has shown remarkable resilience throughout her life, from living in the projects to creating and building projects.

I thank God for my husband and business partner of 43 years for always encouraging and pushing me to the forefront. I started with a triplex and completed over $700 million in real estate transactions. Together, we have over 100 residential properties, in three states and completed our first 74-unit $40 million apartment building from the ground up in September for "grandparents raising their grandchildren." I am also an author, coach, speaker, and philanthropist.

However, the road was and is difficult. This is a male-dominated industry, and I have had to overcome many obstacles throughout my 36-year journey. This story is my testament to the power of resilience and how it can help us overcome even the toughest challenges in life." Most gurus tell you how good real Estate investing is. I am transparent and tell you the Good, Bad and the Ugly.

We bought land in Jacksonville, Florida, for $400k to develop housing. We put up 200k cash and financed 200k with a second mortgage on our primary home. We had not done our due diligence as thoroughly as we should have and had not established relationships with the city's mayor, council members, or players. You must establish relationships to help move you along in any entrepreneurial venture.

The planning and permit process became overwhelming and took longer than expected. The market changed amid all this. Taxes went up, lending dried up, folks began using the land as a trash dump, and fines accumulated. We wound up selling a 400k property for 100k, losing 300K on the deal. This taught me to stay in my lane, and if you still want to do it, partner with someone more experienced than you are. This experience gave me resilience, toughness, grit, determination, persistence, and a never-quit attitude that has served me well.

Remember, life is a school, and we are here to learn. Problems are simply part of the curriculum that appear and fade away, but the lessons we learn will last a lifetime. As one of my mentors said, in this game, you will lose money, but if you win 51% or more of the time, you are ahead of the game. We were knocked down but not out! We took our learning to heart because we wanted to get into development and persisted until we found a partner who bought us into several other deals that made millions.

But how do we find the resilience within?

We must remember that Jesus Himself is a model of resilience (Hebrews 12:1-3). He fought through temptations, persecutions, and crucifixion. As for me I seek God 1st his righteousness and everything else is added unto me! Matthew 6:33

R - Remember your why, build relationships and keep your eye on the prize!

E - Embrace the challenge and not the failure

S –Seek God first and stay positive.

I – Identify your strengths & weaknesses.

L - Learn from your mistakes and look for opportunities.

I – Invest in yourself.

E - Engage with others.

N - Never give up.

C- Choose gratefulness & control what you can

E- Environment- Be the architect and not the victim of your environment.

May you always find the resilience within to overcome any challenge and win!

Janet Tonkins

Janet Tonkins is a real estate developer, investor, coach, author, speaker, and philanthropist affectionately known in her hometown of Baltimore, MD, as "The Cashflow Diva, because she buys houses like women buy shoes." She started in poverty, living in the CCP projects of New Jersey. As a Christian striving to treat everyone the way she wants to be treated, she built a reputation as the "go-to" person in Baltimore for rental properties because of excellence. Her mantra is, "I won't give anyone anything I can't live in myself." She has shown remarkable resilience throughout her life, from living in the projects to building projects.

This mother of three, with her husband and business partner of 43 years, have completed over $700 million in real estate transactions. They have over 100 residential properties in three states and completed their first 74-unit $40 million apartment building for "grandparents raising their grandchildren" in September.

Girl, Get Up

By Rynette Upson-Bush

Then Jesus said to him, "Get up! Pick up your mat and walk."
John 5:8

The last three years of my life have been the worst and the best years of my life. I have lost 21 people in my life that I knew to death, and I lost my dog. My life has been forever changed! It all started when I lost my grandson in a tragic car accident. He was only six and on life support for nine days before they pulled the plug. We donated his organs. He saved six lives, and that's great, but I wish so many days I could have him back. I hadn't had a chance to even grieve his death because my son, his father, was a whole wreck after losing his son, and my family was hurting badly. I had to be the strong one.

On top of this horrific loss that was only the start for what was to come. Death hit my family back-to-back. In 5 weeks, every single week, someone died. My aunt, my uncle, my daddy, another uncle, and one of my friends died one after the other. It was overwhelming. I felt so empty, but I was still trying to move forward with my coaching business, and I was helping people but not helping myself. I was so empty, but I was afraid to stop because I felt in my heart that if I stopped, I wouldn't be able to start again and on top of that, I would have to really face the reality of what was happening in my life if I stopped working. With so much death and darkness, I feared what would happen if I slowed down. I was torn, worn and aged about five years in a couple of months due to the stress and heartache. I ended up in grief recovery for 16 weeks at the suggestion of a friend and therapist. It was a deep dive, but it was necessary to peel back the layers and find myself again.

95

Through the therapy process, as I spilled my guts over the weeks and recalled my life, the therapist helped me uncover that I had been living in grief my entire life. Wow!! I guess I had just been living through it. She said you have fought through a lot but never quit, and you can fight through this pain, too. And guess what I did!

We all have a story. We all have been through some things. It's a part of life whether we like it or not. Too often, we allow ourselves to sit stale, stuck, and stagnant. We ask ourselves, why is this happening to us? We play the blame game. We point fingers and fall into pity parties due to our circumstances.

I know it hurts. I know it's a hard pill to swallow when we go through tough times. I'm not making light of it. I've been in that place, too, trying to get through the trials and tribulations of life. However, our response to situations keeps us stuck and lacking instead of flourishing and prospering. We must decide to get up, bounce back and walk in resilience.

This man who sat at the pool of Bethesda sat there for many years, holding on to this mat. He treasured this mat more than he treasured God. He held on to his mat as if his life depended on it. He sat on that mat and watched the world pass him by. He was so attached to that mat that he couldn't imagine living without it, so when Jesus told him to pick it up and walk, he didn't do it. Like the man at the pool of Bethesda, honey, it's time to pick up your mat and move!

It's time to trust God and let Him carry it all because He can. What's too much for us is nothing for God. God has hope and a great future planned for you. Are you ready to take your mat and walk? Your biggest dreams, visions, and all you want awaits you.

Girl, it's time to get up and be resilient so you can go to your next level!! Pick up that mat, and Let's GO! Whatever you have been through, you can get back up and walk out better and stronger! You are resilient!

Rynette Upson-Bush

Rynette Upson-Bush, aka The Purpose Pusher, is a powerhouse speaker. She is the founder and CEO of The Next Level Nation and Next Level Trippin. Her passion and adoration for helping people have moved her to chase her life's calling to educate, empower and enlighten people, particularly women, on how to see more wealth, success, and happiness in life. Rynette is a speaker, emcee, visibility coach and certified educator. She helps her clients show up for themselves so they can go up and get paid!

Embracing the Journey of Joyful Resilience

By Sunita Uthra

"The greatest glory in living lies not in never falling,
but in rising every time we fall."
Nelson Mandela

"Koi baat nahin, Beta. Phir se karte hain", "It's ok, dear. Let's do this again"—those encouraging words of my parents still ring in my ears. Growing up in India as the eldest of four daughters. I was fortunate to see the remarkable resilience displayed by my parents, who had risen from humble beginnings. They were true trailblazers, overcoming many challenges and instilling in me the values of integrity, determination, honesty, and unwavering commitment to hard work. These values became my guiding stars as I embarked on my career journey. With each milestone I achieved, I felt a profound sense of validation, as if the universe itself affirmed I was on the right path. Awards and recognition came my way, affirming the dedication and effort I poured into my work. It seemed as though my journey was destined for an upward trajectory. However, life has a curious way of testing our resilience when we least expect it.

One seemingly ordinary day, I walked into my office, prepared for another day at work. But ordinary, it was not, as I was informed that my position had been eliminated. In an instant, my world changed, and I felt like I had lost a significant part of my identity, making me question the path I had diligently paved for myself. It was as if I was being put to the ultimate test.

In this unexpected crisis, I found solace and strength in the teachings of my Buddhist faith, which reminded me that challenges are growth opportunities. Embracing this wisdom, I resolved to face this setback with a positive mindset, drawing on the well of potential that lay dormant within me. Rather than succumb to despair, I consciously decided to rise above adversity, much like my parents had done in their own lives. I knew that I had a choice—to let discouragement consume me or to harness my inner strength and embark on a transformative journey of resilience and find my JOY in the midst of adversity.

During this period of uncertainty, I focused on pursuits that had so far lingered on the periphery of my busy life. One such dream was to pen a book—a dream that had patiently awaited its turn on my bucket list. I embarked on a collaborative effort with a remarkable group of women to co-author a book with our learnings and experiences acquired while navigating the complex corporate world, to empower others, especially women, to embrace their unique strengths and persevere in the face of daunting challenges. To our astonishment and delight, it soared to become an Amazon bestseller on its first day of release. It was a testament to the power of resilience and the profound impact that sharing our stories could have on others. I was motivated even more to intensify my efforts of igniting courage within the hearts of aspiring women, and these moments reinforced my belief in the boundless potential of individuals to rise above adversity and emerge stronger, wiser, and more empowered. I found the value of JOY - a compass that guided me through this uncertain phase and will do so for the future.

> **J** - Journey of Growth: I realized that life's journey is a tapestry of good and bad experiences. Resilience is not merely about bouncing back; it's about bouncing forward with newfound strength and purpose. Every challenge presented an opportunity for growth and learning.

> **O** -Optimistic Outlook: Cultivating an optimistic outlook meant acknowledging difficulties and setbacks without losing hope focusing on the positive aspects, even in the face of adversity.

Optimism became the driving force that propelled me forward, with the awareness that joy was integral to the journey itself.

Y - Yield to Self-Compassion: I learned to be kind to myself, treating myself with the same kindness and understanding I would offer to a dear friend. Self-compassion created a safe space for healing and growth, letting me bounce back with greater strength and resilience, even in moments of vulnerability.

As I now navigate through the ever-testing waters of life, hope shines brightly within me, illuminating the path forward. I carry the wisdom of embracing setbacks as opportunities to grow and become a better version of myself.

I am ready to fully embrace my journey of joyful resilience.

Sunita Uthra

Sunita Uthra is a global technology leader with an illustrious career across several Fortune 500 companies. Her innovative and trans-formative approach has driven business success, fostering revenue growth and operational excellence. Beyond her professional achievements, Sunita is dedicated to using emerging technologies for societal benefit, empowering women in STEM, and mentoring the next generation of tech leaders. Her commitment to positive change is apparent through advisory roles with non-profit organizations "Humans for AI" and "Entertainment 2 Affect Change." She co-authored the Amazon Bestseller "Letters to my Corporate Sisters: Stories of Endurance, Elevation, and Encouragement" and was featured on the podcast "Extraordinary Women in Technology."

Sunita's impact was recognized with the 2023 Technology Leadership award by "Empowered Women of the World." With a Master's degree in Computer Applications from Thapar Engineering College, India, and currently pursuing an MBA at Wake Forest University, she firmly believes in continuous education for personal and professional growth.

Beauty for Ashes

By Bridget Washington

"To console those who mourn in Zion, To give them beauty for ashes, The oil of joy for mourning, The garment of praise for the spirit of heaviness; That they may be called trees of righteousness, The planting of the Lord, that He may be glorified."
Isaiah 61:3

BOOM! As I sat at my desk in my home office on October 17th, 2022, I wondered what loud noise I heard that seemed to come out of the kitchen. I knew my husband was working from the table; I thought his computer monitor was accidentally knocked off the table. I was wrong, as, to my shock, he was face down on the floor unconscious. I ran over to him, called out to him, and nudged him. He regained consciousness, wondering what happened. He sat up, regained his composure, and walked over to the couch to sit down. Leading to this point, he had what he thought was a severe sinus and ear infection, which gave him a clogged sensation in his ears along with slight jolts of pain. I told him it was time to go to the hospital. What was discovered once we got there would change the trajectory of our lives.

Tests. Bloodwork. Cat scan. Waiting. The doctor walks in the ER room. "Sir, we got the results back from the cat scan. You have a tumor in your brain, and unfortunately, you will not be going home today. You will be admitted. We looked at the image of the scan and looked at each other, perplexed. My husband then shifts gears and says, "What's next?"

The Valley moment had officially begun. Know that in valley moments, you must rely on the strength of God, and your faith muscles will be put front and center on display. My spouse would go on later that week to have a craniotomy to remove as much of the tumor as possible without causing any major aftereffects or complications. Then, as the doctors suspected, he was officially diagnosed with Glioblastoma Multiforme Grade 4, a highly aggressive brain cancer with no cure and a dismal extended living rate. As we walked the course of treatment (two craniotomies, radiation, chemotherapy, physical therapy), God mandated me to switch gears from loving wife to educated advocate and caregiver. God specifically told me my assignment in that season was make sure he is prepared to meet Me, because I will not heal him on this earth. I need you to be obedient to this. Okay, Lord.... let's go.

No matter how hard or scary it may seem or how unknown the circumstances or outcome may be, obedience matters. Obedience captures God's attention, and He will cover and keep you in ways you can't begin to imagine.

As I assumed the caregiver role, I had to continually renew my mindset. Speaking positive affirmations over myself and my husband's mindset, sickness, and day-to-day living was key. The disease began to eat away at his mindset as he was diagnosed with Aphasia, his vision began to deteriorate, and multiple mobility issues began to surface. It was a trying time, as I attributed this to the Aphasia. Simple conversations were often unclear and misunderstood, resulting in conflict and frustration. I cried out to God to ask for one simple thing: peace. He granted it continually.

Peace is the driver of pressing through every trial and tribulation in your life. Peace also fuels your strength to overcome. Hold on to your peace. Change is coming!

After ten months, my husband passed away on August 22nd, 2022. As difficult as it was, I stayed the course of my assignment, and he was ushered into the presence of the Lord. During my grief, God smothered me with supernatural peace and released me to move on to the next season of my life. Many tell me I don't look like what I have gone through. I look at it as God's divine grace over my life, and He continues to bless me, open doors, and I will ride this life happy, full of joy, favor and success until the wheels fall off.

Expect your rainbow after the storm. Embrace everything that you went through while in the storm – those foggy nights, torrential downpours, gusty winds, and catastrophic flooding. One thing I know for sure – the Lord is a promise keeper. There is a rainbow with your name on it, and it is God's promise of restoration, blessings, and elevation for your life. He will grant you beauty for ashes.

Bridget Washington

Bridget Washington is a passionate servant leader with a unique ability to peel the layers of mediocrity and build up individuals to reach their fullest potential. The Maxwell Leadership Certified Leadership Development Speaker, Coach, and Trainer is the founder of BriMari Marie) Global LLC, a Personal Development and Leadership company. Bridget is the host of Living a Fanatical Life Podcast, "Where Faith, Empowerment, & Purpose Collide". A prolific writer, she is the author of "Fanatical: Living a God Inspired Life You Are Crazy About", the visionary behind the compilation "Fanatical: 13 Trailblazers Who are Living Bold, Inspired Lives," and the coming book release, "Fanatical Faith." Excited about helping transform everyday lives from ordinary to extraordinary, her motto is "Always Live Fanatical!"

The Game of Life

By Angela Williams

"In the game of life, resilience is our most powerful cheat code. It's not about avoiding the hard levels, it's about taking them head-on and moving forward, one small victory at a time."
Angela Williams

At 28, I was catapulted into a reality that felt more like a video game than actual life. I was a young mother of four energetic boys, each of them my heart and soul. Among them, my youngest, born in 2002, was grappling with a level much more difficult than the rest of us, battling the daily obstacles presented by Cerebral Palsy. His joy and spirit were like power-ups, pushing us forward and inspiring us daily.

Every day was a new level, a fresh quest. From therapy sessions, school runs, meals to be cooked, and a house to be cleaned, it was a non-stop, full-throttle race against the clock. It was exhausting, but each power-up moment, each little victory, and each love-filled gaze was worth the grind.

A formidable boss level presented itself in the middle of this real-life game. My rock, my cheerleader, my mother, was fighting a fierce battle against breast cancer. I witnessed her strength and courage as she faced each treatment, each setback, and each win. Her endurance was like an unbeatable high score that kept us going. In March 2007, after an intense battle, she lost her fight, leaving an indescribable void in our lives.

Her absence hit like a sudden glitch in the game, a wave of sorrow that threatened to stall our progress. Depression crept in like a shadowy adversary, darkening the game screen of my life. The battle against this unseen enemy was uncharted territory.

However, in my solitude, I found strength. The echo of my boys' laughter, the memory of my mother's resilience, and the smiles of my youngest sparked light in the darkness. Their belief in me was the cheat code I needed to push through the levels of despair.

I understood then that this game called life was not about avoiding challenges but navigating them. I realized every hurdle was a chance to level up and discover untapped strength and resilience. And in this discovery, I found my power, my ability to forge ahead, no matter how intense the level.

Takeaway Tips:

- Embrace Solitude: You might find the cheat code to your challenges in those quiet moments. Embrace it and let it strengthen you.
- Love is Your Power-Up: The love of your family can help you power through the toughest levels. Use it as your motivation.
- Face Your Boss Levels: Every challenge you encounter is a chance to level up. Don't avoid them, face them head-on.
- Don't be Afraid to Ask for Help: Remember there's always a support team even if you're playing solo. Reach out when you need to. It's not a sign of defeat.
- Celebrate Your Wins: Every win, big or small, is an achievement. Celebrate them. They're proof of your resilience.
- Self-Care is Important: Remember to pause the game occasionally to take care of your mental and physical health.
- Every Game Has Its Ups and Downs: Life, like a game, has good levels and bad ones. Understand this and remember that no level is unbeatable.
- Resilience is Pushing Forward: Resilience isn't about not facing difficult levels; it's about pushing forward despite them. Your journey is a testament to that strength and will inspire others in their own game of life.

Angela Williams

Angela Williams, a dedicated mother, best-selling author, and Goal Success Coach, symbolizes resilience, personal growth, and unwavering support for others. Her own life, enriched by deep and meaningful lessons, has shaped her into a passionate Mental Resilience Coach. Her purpose is to empower women, aiding them in overcoming adversity, finding balance, and embracing joy. Angela's influence extends beyond coaching, captivating audiences as an eloquent emcee and keynote speaker.

Her courage is exemplified in her victorious battle against breast cancer, an experience that solidified her dedication to fostering hope and resilience in others. Angela promotes aromatherapy as an Independent Scentsy Consultant, advocates for wellness as a Certified SPIN instructor, and a BODi Coach. Angela's inspiring journey is a testament to the power of resilience and the capacity to flourish amidst challenges. Connect with Angela through email at awresiliencecoach@gmail.com or follow her on Instagram at todays_vibe4.0.

Made in the USA
Middletown, DE
29 October 2023

41474794R00062